TREASURES OF TALIESIN

SEVENTY-SIX UNBUILT DESIGNS

FRANK LLOYD WRIGHT

 THE PRESS AT CALIFORNIA STATE UNIVERSITY, FRESNO

TREASURES OF TALIESIN

SEVENTY-SIX UNBUILT DESIGNS

BRUCE BROOKS PFEIFFER

SOUTHERN ILLINOIS UNIVERSITY PRESS ■ CARBONDALE AND EDWARDSVILLE

Printed in Japan

Edited by Susan H. Wilson
Designed by Susan Jacobs Lockhart
Production supervised by Kathleen Giencke
90 89 88 87 86 85 6 5 4 3 2 1

Library of Congress Cataloging in Publication Data

Pfeiffer, Bruce Brooks.
   Treasures of Taliesin, 76 unbuilt designs of Frank Lloyd Wright.

   1. Wright, Frank Lloyd, 1867–1959.   2. Architectural drawing—20th century—United States.   3. Taliesin West (Scottsdale, Ariz.)   I. Wright, Frank Lloyd, 1867–1959.   II. Title.   III. Title: Treasures of Taliesin, seventy-six unbuilt designs of Frank Lloyd Wright.
NA2707.W74P44   1986   720'.22'2   85-2360
ISBN 0-8093-1235-2

Orders should be addressed to:
Southern Illinois University Press
P.O. Box 3697
Carbondale, IL 62902–3697

Dedicated to William Wesley Peters

CONTENTS

This book presents 106 drawings for designs of Frank Lloyd Wright, many of which are published here for the first time. Frank Lloyd Wright designed over one thousand structures, nearly 45 percent of which were constructed—a very high percentage as architectural commissions go. Yet the architect believed that his unbuilt designs were the most interesting of his works. They undoubtedly reveal the diverse genius of the man who conceived them.

In architecture, the word *project* refers to work that is designed but not built. Designs that are constructed are called *executed*. Mr. Wright's projects have remained unexecuted for reasons that range from the dramatic to the absurd. It is tragic that projects so brilliantly conceived, so timeless, should remain unbuilt to this day.

Frank Lloyd Wright never designed in theory, just for the sake of designing something. Each project was intended for construction as an executed work of architecture. Some of these projects here rank among his grandest conceptions, such as the Monona Terrace Civic Center (plates 61a, 61b) and the Pittsburgh Point Park Civic Center (plates 43a–43d). In the Mile High skyscraper, the principles employed in his design represent a culmination of major phases of his work. He traced the roots of the Mile High back to the windmill tower, Romeo and Juliet, that he built for his aunts' Hillside Home School in 1896. He traced its branching out to St. Mark's Tower of 1929, with its taproot foundation, which he finally built as the research tower for the Johnson Company in Racine, Wisconsin. But the fullest flowering of all these ideas and structural concepts came together in this startling design for the Mile High, an office building of 528 stories, lightweight, slender, graceful, human (plates 64a, 64b).

In addition to the designs made for buildings, Mr. Wright also created designs for furnishings, decorative arts, landscaping, and other aspects associated with his structures. He often described his buildings as "organic architecture," distinguishing them from other contemporary structures and from the imitative traditional buildings under construction during his long and prolific career. In organic architecture, all the parts are related to each other and to the whole. This sense of the total product, related and woven into one entity, is possible only when the architect has the ability to design not only the building itself but all its component parts. Where the client could afford this total design, the Frank Lloyd Wright building sings with a harmonious beauty rare in the world of architecture. Midway Gardens, the Larkin Building (plate 72), Fallingwater, and the Johnson Administration Building are vigorous examples of works that bear Mr. Wright's signature from the overall structure to the minutest detail. Smaller, less expensive buildings, like the houses for John Pew, Frank Sander, and Gerald Tonkens, have the same unified quality.

THE DRAWINGS

The actual process of design was a very swift one for Frank Lloyd Wright. He thought out a new work entirely in his head before he touched pencil to paper. Once the design, including all the details, was clearly formulated, he would go to the drafting room and start to draw. Those first sketches of his are, of course, the most priceless of all his architectural drawings. From them, we, his apprentices, began to make more detailed drawings. First there were the renderings or presentation drawings, which Mr. Wright colored and worked on himself in preparation for showing to his client. The final stage, the working drawings, were the actual documents from which the building was constructed.

When we started photographing the drawings for this book, the results were both revealing and exciting. We soon found that in examining each work, we were looking not at mere images of buildings but at the actual buildings themselves. The wealth of detail and the architect's use of space and line imbue the drawings with a life of their own.

That the illustrations show the genius of one of the greatest architects of this century is self-evident. Less obvious perhaps but implicit in the character of the work and borne out in the text is the fierce integrity of their creator. Many of these projects were not built because Mr. Wright consistently refused to compromise his work and its principles. He would rather see a project dropped and his drawings returned to the files at Taliesin than sacrifice its quality and beauty to please a client, a contractor, or a building commissioner. By holding fast to his principles, he certainly lost work that would have ordinarily come his way. But he never showed remorse or regret for having held to his deep sense of what was right in architecture. To those of us who lived at Taliesin while he was alive and working he said, "You must be in love with architecture. Forget it as a profession. It will soon come to you in that sense. But be in love with it. Architecture is a dedication to something holy, to which I render my service."

We at the Frank Lloyd Wright Foundation are gratified to note a growing interest not only in the study and appreciation of Frank Lloyd Wright's work but also in the construction of the projects lying dormant on paper—these vibrant, youthful, and creative designs ready to spring to three-dimensional life.

Bruce Brooks Pfeiffer   Taliesin West   January 24, 1985

Edward C. Waller, one of Frank Lloyd Wright's first clients, was a prominent realtor and developer in Chicago and the surrounding suburbs, commissioning Mr. Wright for various private homes as well as apartment buildings. Many commissions were completed, though some remained projects—usually the more ambitious and extensive ones.

After a client received a set of plans with "Frank Lloyd Wright, Architect" on them, he or she faced an ordeal: seeking the banker's approval. In the late 1890s and early 1900s, this invariably posed a problem. Bankers, by nature, are usually conservative, and they were even more so then. When it came to architecture they responded only to what they had seen around them—traditional styles and embellishments and the conventional means of putting them up. For this reason, many of the larger schemes that required extensive bank financing were not built if Mr. Wright was the architect. Adding to the problem was the Columbian Exposition in 1893, which created a flood of classicism that covered not only the Midwest but inundated the nation as a whole.

Two years after this architectural deluge, Mr. Waller asked Mr. Wright to design an amusement park for a small lake, Wolf Lake, south of Chicago on the Illinois / Indiana state line. The drawing for this park (plate 1) exudes joy and activity. Lagoons for bathing and boating are incorporated within the scheme as integral features of the plan. Avenues, promenades, casinos, dance halls, and concessions are placed along a half-circle mall and its extended wings.

The plan of the work reveals an important breakthrough. The natural, half-circle inlet of the building site determines the main design contour of the proposed park. This example of land planning was a startling concept for 1895. Decades were to pass before the terms "land planning" and "site planning" were in use. Here, the land serves as the determining factor of the design itself. From the wooded inlet the park grows out gracefully in projecting arms into the water beyond.

Although Waller did not build this park or another one that Mr. Wright designed for him at Cheltenham Beach in Chicago, six years later, his son, Edward, Jr., built the famed Midway Gardens—a restaurant, cabaret, summer and winter garden in south Chicago designed by Mr. Wright. Midway Gardens was constructed about twenty years after Wolf Park was designed, but it too was ill-fated. Prohibition set in and ruined the establishment as a bar and cabaret. The Gardens were torn down some twenty years after they were built. But so well built were they, so firmly constructed of reinforced concrete and brick, that three demolition companies went bankrupt in the attempt to demolish them.

That dilemma illustrates yet another important factor in the work of Frank Lloyd Wright: the manner in which he regarded the art of architecture. For him a building should be designed and built to last at least three hundred years. No one has the right, Mr. Wright believed, to erect a building that is shoddy or cheap, that will not endure. Yet much architecture built today is constructed with hardly more than stage-setting stability.

YAHARA BOATHOUSE, MADISON, WISCONSIN, 1902

The Yahara Boathouse (plate 2) was intended for the racing crew of the University of Wisconsin at Madison. The city and the campus are endowed with four lakes, two large and two small. Boating and sailing were familiar pastimes for the citizens of Madison as well as for the students of the university.

The long, sleek lines of the proposed Yahara Boathouse reflect its function as storage for the long, sleek rowing shells. Mr. Wright's boyhood friend, Robert Lamp, was a cripple whom Mr. Wright had befriended and defended during their high school years. Lamp's great passion was boating. He was responsible for the city of Madison building Mr. Wright's boathouse on Lake Mendota. The Yahara Boathouse was also sponsored and promoted by Lamp, but to no avail. The university authorities must have been shocked by the streamlined clarity of this design in 1902; the boathouse plan was rejected.

Two years later, however, Mr. Wright designed and built a home for Lamp in Madison. He situated the house in such a way that, from the garden roof deck, Robbie (as he called his friend) could watch the boat races on both

lakes, the house lot being on the isthmus between them. As early as 1902 the houses he designed, both built and unbuilt, reflected his innate ability to blend the building with the site. He maintained that the more varied, the more complex, and even the more difficult the site, the better the house he could design for it. Out of the very idiosyncracies of the topography and terrain he derived his inspiration.

Mr. Wright loved the way in which Madison was situated, with its four lakes. He grew up in this area and spent both his high school and college years in Madison. But the city soon turned its back on the fortunate location of these lakes, and the lake fronts became "back yards." In 1938, however, Mr. Wright designed a civic center for Lake Monona issuing from the heart of the city out over the lake (plates 22a, 22b). The project for this center was dropped in 1939, was revived again in 1955 (plates 61a, 61b), and was set aside once again. Madison was fated not to have one of the most beautiful buildings ever designed by Mr. Wright.

HIGHLAND PARK HOUSE, HIGHLAND PARK, ILLINOIS, 1904
H. J. ULLMAN HOUSE, OAK PARK, ILLINOIS, 1904

Early in his career, from 1893 to 1910, Frank Lloyd Wright designed houses primarily for suburban or urban lots, albeit on the prairie with vast open spaces around them or in suburbs that were still countrified. The prairie in and around Chicago was flat and monotonous, and to give the greatest possible expression to human life lived in this environment, he raised the living area up off the damp ground, placed the formerly dug-in basement on ground level, and extended, wherever possible, a sense of the horizontal line. Everything about those early "prairie" houses was broad, horizontal, generous, ground-loving, and sheltered. He believed that the American family should live in close relationship to the landscape and countryside wherever possible, yet sheltered and protected from the elements both in summer and in winter. This belief gave rise to his use of the open-swinging window, set under a wide eave and protected by it. From the beginning of his work he established a sense of continuity between the interior and the exterior, often referring to that continuity as "not being able to tell when the outside leaves off and the inside begins."

The sketch of the Highland Park House (plate 3a) shows how he placed a house of that era in a wooded glen. The proximity of the foliage to the house illustrates how the dwelling and its setting coexisted as an organic whole.

The prairie houses Mr. Wright designed and built became the models from which all contemporary domestic architecture derives its inspiration or imitates its effects. The "ranch-colonial," the "open plan," even the Midwest bungalow all grew out of that early work.

3b

The house for H. J. Ullman (plate 3b) is an appropriate house for the Midwest prairie, and the perspective drawing clearly demonstrates the manner in which the main living area is raised off the damp ground. Overhanging eaves protect the window areas, and the fireplaces are grouped beneath one generous chimney.

The water table, shown in the drawing as a white, poured-concrete line supporting the red brick walls, is left intentionally exposed and emphasized. This groundline is extremely important in Mr. Wright's work, because of the way in which he "married" the building to the terrain. Traditional houses of the same era had their basement windows peeping up above the groundline to permit light into the cellar below. This unsightly feature was then masked by means of dense foliage and shrubbery. Mr. Wright found the solution of foundation planting, as it is called, most odious. It brings moisture and clinging dampness up to the base of the building, an undesirable element for the structure itself, encouraging rot and decay. In his work, the line where the building meets the ground is an attractive feature; foundation planting would needlessly obliterate it. In the perspective of this drawing, he has featured that groundline in a clean and uncluttered way.

Planting and landscaping, always desirable in a dwelling, are treated here as accenting features to the home, part of the building. They serve as a gentle companion to it for the pleasure of its occupants. No building of his was ever without flowers and foliage. In his interiors, he specified large, generous bowls of fresh flowers, as well as special places, integral with the architecture, where growing plants should be cultivated.

In 1910–11 Frank Lloyd Wright lived in Fiesole, a small hillside town near Florence. He was preparing his Wasmuth portfolio at that time. Entitled *Ausgeführte Bauten und Entwürfe von Frank Lloyd Wright (The Executed Buildings and the Projects of Frank Lloyd Wright)*, it would be published in that year by the distinguished publishing house of Ernst Wasmuth in Berlin. The portfolio was destined to be a landmark in the history and growth of modern architecture in Europe. His son Lloyd Wright and draftsman Taylor Woolley assisted him in the project.

Also with him was his companion, Mamah Borthwick Cheney, and it was for her and for himself that Mr. Wright designed a studio-villa (plate 4). The villa for Fiesole shows his thorough understanding of how to build in this Italian setting. The building is brought directly to the street edge, as a wall, permitting an enclosed and secluded garden within. The roof line seen over the street wall is actually set back on the other side of the garden, while a projecting section comes to the wall with its grouping of three windows and a decorative frieze above.

Mr. Wright returned to America before actually building the studio-residence, and many years later, in 1957, he proposed the same design for an American client living in Cuernavaca, Mexico. Unfortunately, like the original for Fiesole, it was never built.

Mr. Wright's flight to Europe with Mrs. Cheney, wife of his client E. H. Cheney, fomented a scandal that haunted him for many years. Unable to live a lie, he realized that after eighteen years his marriage to his wife, Catherine, had become increasingly difficult—virtually a failure from his point of view. And he had fallen in love with the talented Mrs. Cheney. He acted upon that realization, left his wife and six children, and took Mrs. Cheney to Italy to work. Several of his clients helped him financially, though they believed that his taking Mrs. Cheney abroad was most unethical. It was certainly unconventional and controversial. But of course he was, from the very start of his life, an unconventional and controversial person. At the same time, he came from a stringently puritanical Welsh background. He innately abhorred immorality. Mr. Wright was the son and the grandson of ministers, and his mother was an educator. He believed strongly in the American family, almost as a sacred unit, essential to the healthy growth and development of society. The plans of his dwellings made that belief evident: the central core, the very heart of the home is the fireplace hearth with its welcoming and comforting fire burning deep within a generous masonry mass, flanked by seats for family and guests. His sojourn in Europe must therefore have caused him much pain and concern, having left hearth, home, and children behind. We read in his autobiography of some of that pain; at times it became nothing less than anguish.

Three clients came to his aid in these difficult years, and to those three clients he dedicated his Wasmuth portfolio: "Charles E. Roberts, Francis W. Little, and Darwin D. Martin—three American men of affairs—who have believed in and befriended this work when natural opposition from without and inherent faults within threatened to make an end of it. Without their faith and help this work would never have reached its present development."

FOR THE ARCHITECT
TIVE STUDY FLORENCE 1910

Sherman Booth's property in Glencoe, Illinois, was one of the first really magnificent opportunities that Frank Lloyd Wright had to create a design for a varied topography in a wooded glen split by a deep ravine. The approach to the house (plate 5) is via a bridge over a gorge, leading directly to the building itself. A two-story living room extends down into the ravine, and wings spread out from the central living room core to accommodate other rooms at various levels.

Although the most striking feature of the design is undoubtedly the treatment of the ravine, Mr. Wright has treated the access and approach to it in much the same manner as he did the waterfall at Fallingwater. It is done with intricate subtlety. Crossing the bridge, one gets only a glimpse of the glen, but once inside the house the beauty of the ravine and its natural landscape is revealed as part of the interior of the house itself. The entrance to the house is likewise treated as a series of approaches, not as a sudden confrontation. This is generally true of all of Mr. Wright's interiors. Throughout the major part of Western architecture, a certain formality, evident as the major-minor axis, makes the plan evident upon first sight of the building. Everything is centered and balanced, precisely laid out right to left and left to right. Upon entering the governor's mansion of one of the East Coast states, Mr. Wright remarked: "Ah yes, I know the plan: stairway to the right and to the left, main hall on this side, dining room on that side, ladies lounge beneath the right stairway, gentlemen's beneath the left stairway. It is all apparent the moment you step from the portico into the front reception area."

In a Frank Lloyd Wright residence, the visitor is led into a room by an almost circuitous route. Anticipation is aroused. One turns a corner, goes from a low area to a high area, perhaps turns again, and then, suddenly, the objective is attained, the main living space is found. In the case of the Booth residence, the entrance proceeds from a roofed area at the end of the bridge to a small entry. A turn to the left and then a turn to the right places the visitor under a low balcony, and only once again, on the right, does one see the full room with its two-story glass doors leading out to the terrace that borders the ravine.

The grammar (the basic architectural design and treatment of materials employed) of this house is similar to that of Mr. Wright's own home, Taliesin, in Wisconsin. Both works were designed in the same year, 1911. Booth, Mr. Wright's attorney, never built this house for reasons that are lost in time. However, Mr. Wright designed another home for him that was built, along with four smaller houses for resale and a charming bridge over the ravine.

FRANK LLOYD WRIGHT GOETHE STREET HOUSE
CHICAGO, ILLINOIS, 1911

Upon returning from Florence in 1911, Frank Lloyd Wright decided not to go back to his home and studio in Oak Park, near Chicago. He had made an irrevocable break with his wife and family, had closed the studio, and had terminated his work. One of the first things he did upon arriving in Chicago was to make designs for the remodeling of his former home and studio to provide for three apartments that his wife could rent out as a means of income.

For himself, his return after one year's work on the Wasmuth portfolio in Florence meant a totally new direction for his personal and for his professional life. He had long kept an office in Chicago, which he now opened again as he became established in the Midwest. But his architectural practice grew slowly as a result of his two-year absence.

The townhouse (plate 6) to be built on Goethe Street (Mr. Wright greatly admired the poet Goethe) was to be his home and office in Chicago. In the center of the building rises a tall loggia court, upon which all the other rooms open. Skylights atop the loggia fill the court with light. The walls are surfaced in exquisite, large Japanese screens that he purchased. Part of the structure is reserved as a private residence. The part facing the street contains offices, a reception area, and a large drafting room for his architectural practice.

In that same year he built a home for his mother, Anna Lloyd Wright, on the family land near Spring Green, Wisconsin. Anna Wright lived in Chicago, but this new cottage was to be her summer home near the Hillside Home School, which she and her two sisters had founded in 1885. Mr. Wright had returned from Florence with Mrs. Mamah Cheney, and they needed a place to live and work until the Goethe Street home was built. His mother suggested they take over the cottage in Spring Green. She would be perfectly content, she told him, to live at the Hillside Home School a mile away, where she had already lived for much of her life.

He accepted the offer and moved from Chicago to Spring Green, back to the valley of his childhood days on the farm. He called the cottage "Taliesin"—a Welsh name meaning "Shining Brow"—because the house was built on the brow of a hill. Taliesin was also the name of a Druid bard who sang of the fine arts in the sixth century A.D. By late summer, Taliesin was complete, but Mr. Wright still maintained an architectural office in Orchestra Hall in Chicago. Unfortunately, the cost of building the townhouse on Goethe Street became an additional expense he could not afford. The Chicago studio-residence therefore remained only a project.

ODAWARA HOTEL, NEAR KAMAKURA, JAPAN, 1917

Aizaku Hayashi, the general manager of the Imperial Hotel in Tokyo, was chiefly responsible for Frank Lloyd Wright's receiving the commission to build the new Imperial Hotel. As early as 1913, he wrote to Mr. Wright telling him that he was pleased that the job was to be his. Mr. Wright made a trip to Tokyo about that time, and the next year the commission was formally confirmed. The hotel was financed mainly by Baron Okura, representing his own interests and also those of the Imperial Household. Over the years, other entrepreneurs bought out both parties and ownership of the hotel passed into the private sector. It was demolished in 1968 in favor of a skyscraper-type hotel on the same site.

Hayashi left the employ of the hotel when the original ownership was transferred, and Mr. Wright made this sketch (plate 7) for him for another hotel, the Odawara Hotel, near Kamakura, a famous Buddhist shrine. The building was never built, primarily because the expected financing never materialized. Few drawings of it exist today. Most of them were lost during the war years when they were stored in the Tokyo office of Mr. Wright's principal Japanese colleague, architect Arata Endo. The perspective presented here shows the graceful manner in which the building intermingled with a forest and a steep hillside.

It was creations such as the Odawara Hotel that prompted Endo to send Mr. Wright the following suggestion, after the devastating Tokyo earthquake of 1923: "Now your chance is here. You will be received here now with admiration and appreciation—late, yes, but not too late. The whole city is at your disposal. Your work here has been prepared for you. You will have more appreciation now than in America. Therefore you had best come here where it is more worthwhile to plant your footsteps than in Los Angeles—don't you think? With this hope and ever increasing love."

Endo and Hayashi remained Mr. Wright's lifelong friends. The moment World War II ended, Mr. Wright sent money to them for help and medication. Both men were elderly and unwell; Mr. Wright invited them to come to Taliesin with their families to spend the rest of their lives, should they wish. They chose to remain in their native land, and their deaths a few years later robbed Mr. Wright of two of his dearest friends. But the sons of both men came as students to the Taliesin Fellowship, and Raku Endo remains to this day a loyal alumnus practicing architecture in Tokyo.

Sometime during 1916, the Spaulding brothers, John S. and William T., invited Frank Lloyd Wright to visit them at their summer home in Pride's Crossing on Boston's North Shore. They had been told that Mr. Wright had begun to amass a fine collection of Japanese prints, and the Spauldings themselves were eager to start a collection of their own. John and his wife had first discovered Japanese prints some years before during a trip to Japan, had brought some examples back to the States, and were now eager to collect in earnest.

Mr. Wright had been buying Japanese prints since his first trip to Japan in 1904. When he finally received the commission to build the Imperial Hotel in Tokyo in 1913, he embarked upon a series of voyages to Japan which would keep him out of the United States for the better part of each year from 1916 to 1922.

The Japanese prints were from the ukiyo-e movement, an art form representing the "floating world," the world of everyday life, superbly executed by such masters as Utamaro, Hokusai, and Hiroshige. Great collections of these artists were being formed in Europe, and the French Impressionists drew much of their inspiration from them. The posters of Henri de Toulouse-Lautrec in particular owe much to the Japanese print. Mr. Wright claimed that the print taught him the "elimination of the insignificant." Simplicity of line, the almost abstract quality of visual effects, the simple and yet ingenious use of color and tone, the absence of dimension and shadow, and the absence of trying to achieve a three-dimensional image on a primarily two-dimensional medium were all attributes of the Japanese print that Mr. Wright deeply admired. He wrote eloquently about their intrinsic beauty.

The Spaulding Collection was one that he shopped for and purchased during his eight years in Japan. The Buckingham Collection in Chicago and the Mansfield Collection at the Metropolitan Museum in New York were also accumulated by him. By the time Mr. Wright completed his work on the Imperial Hotel, he had become the leading purchaser in Japan of not only Japanese prints but also all types of oriental art, both Japanese and Chinese, including screens, lacquer, bronzes, ceramics, embroidery, and sculpture in wood, stone, and cast metal—Mr. Wright invested most of the nearly half-million-dollar commission paid to him for the Imperial Hotel in his own collection. In addition, he received other sums from various collectors in the United States.

Of all the collections in America and Europe, the Spaulding was the finest, and to house and exhibit it Mr. Wright designed a gallery for downtown Boston (plate 8). The section drawing speaks for itself. It demonstrates the manner in which the prints are stored then removed from the narrow flat drawers and placed on the easels above. Special architectural features hold statuary, objects of fine art, plants, and flowers. In the end, the Spauldings decided, however, to give their collection to the Museum of Fine Arts in Boston, where it can be seen to this day. The proposed gallery exists only as a project.

When Mr. Wright first met the Spaulding brothers there arose the question of his commission as their purchasing agent. Asked just what his commission would be, in percentages, time, and costs, Mr. Wright replied that he would send the prints on to Boston from Tokyo, keeping some for himself as he went along. "That doesn't seem a very businesslike approach, Mr. Wright," John Spaulding said. "I know," said Mr. Wright, "but after all, I am not a businessman."

Mr. Wright used to tell the story of how he came to Boston when the collection arrived, and he, the Spauldings, and Frederick William Gookin (the leading Japanese print expert in America) sat down together to open the crates and examine the prints.

For three days we laid out prints and prints and more prints until neither the Spauldings nor Gookin could believe their eyes. Even to me it seemed like some fantastic dream. Sated with riches in the most exquisite graphic art on earth, after three days at a marvelous feast we all sat back, marveled, and rested. . . . After luncheon we went out for a drive in the new Spaulding Stearns-Knight—top down. I was sitting on the rear seat between John and William Spaulding. Not going very fast, enjoying the relaxation, we were passing school grounds, boys playing ball there, when I heard the crack of a bat on the ball: a square hit. I glanced up just in time to see the ball sailing over us. Instinctively I leaped up, reached for the ball, caught it, and threw it back into the game. "Well!" said William Spaulding in astonishment. "So that is it! Well, Mr. Wright, I now know how you got those prints! It's all clear at last!

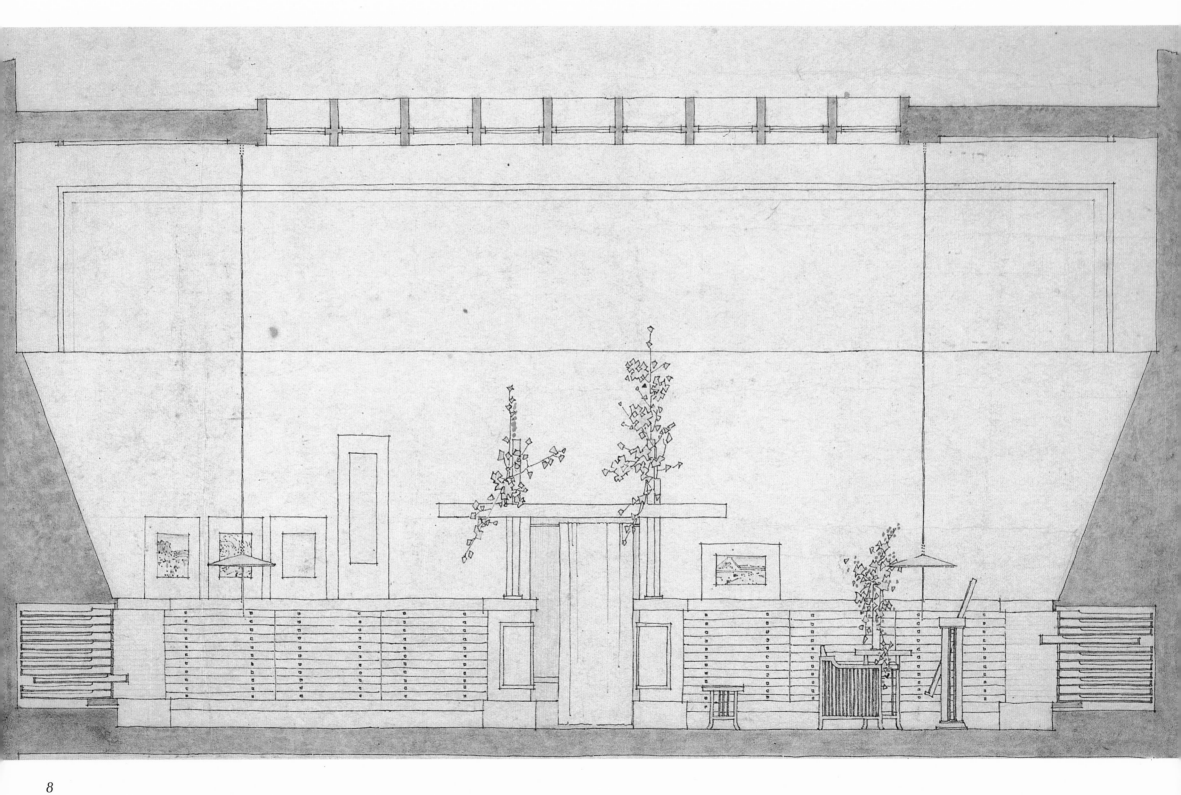

9a

THEATRE FOR ALINE BARNSDALL, LOS ANGELES, CALIFORNIA
1915–1920

A misconception exists concerning the work of Frank Lloyd Wright before and after 1910. The break is obvious because it coincides with the time that he closed his Oak Park studio, went to Europe to prepare a monograph of his work for the German publishing house of Ernst Wasmuth, and then returned to take up residence on his ancestral property in southern Wisconsin, where he built his home and studio, Taliesin, in 1911.

Many theorize that the work following his return to the United States was neither as productive nor as creative as the work from 1893 to 1909. This assumption is incorrect in every way. True, the amount of constructed work tapered off, owing mainly to his being in Japan again and again from 1916 to 1922. There were few American clients during those years, but there was a great deal of work. Two commissions were very sizable jobs: Midway Gardens in Chicago and the Imperial Hotel in Tokyo. Those were in construction, one following the other, from 1913 to 1922. Meanwhile, during his stay in California, he worked for Aline Barnsdall in Los Angeles. Her projects entailed a large theatre, a smaller theatre, three residences, shops, and housing projects. The four famous concrete block houses for Mrs. George Millard, Samuel Freeman, John Storer, and Charles Ennis were also under construction in greater Los Angeles during that period.

A little known work that was begun in 1915 and was expanded in 1917 was his design for the American Ready Cut System houses. Some of these homes were built in the Milwaukee area around 1917, and others are still being discovered in Iowa, Minnesota, and other midwestern states. The file on these prefabricated houses is the largest in the Taliesin archives, with several hundred completed working drawings.

Furthermore, in the ten-year period between 1924 and 1934, between the block houses and Fallingwater, there was an enormous volume of work created but not constructed. The Depression came in during those years, curtailing most building that was not government-sponsored. Yet those years witnessed some of the most innovative designs Mr. Wright ever created, and for all manner of buildings: commercial, residential, civic, and private.

Important unexecuted projects include the Tahoe Summer Colony—a group of cottages and floating cabins for Emerald Bay, Tahoe, California (plates 11a, 11b), San Marcos-in-the-Desert (plates 16a–16c), the Rosenwald School (plate 18), and his designs for the 1931 Chicago World's Fair (plate 19).

The years from 1910 to 1935 reveal a quarter of a century of a continual creative surge of new work and new ideas. A motivating force were the commissions proposed to him by the volatile Aline Barnsdall. These began with her request for a theatre in 1914 (plate 9a).

By the time Mr. Wright returned from his third trip to Japan in 1914, he was well aware of the Japanese dramatic arts, especially the Kabuki theatre. Part of the design of the stage of the Kabuki theatre utilizes a revolving stage, set on a great drum turned by several strong men below, the slow-paced revolutions changing the scene while it is virtually in process. Another feature of the Japanese theatre that appealed to Mr. Wright was the musicians' balcony, above the stage and over to the side, with the sound coming through a latticed screen wall.

In his design for the Imperial Hotel, Mr. Wright planned a theatre with the traditional revolving stage. When he designed his theatre for Miss Barnsdall in Los Angeles, he went even farther in theatre design by abolishing the proscenium. The stage and the audience are thus more closely linked together. He referred to traditional theatre design as one in which the audience sat in one box looking at the performance going on in another box. The principal thrust of his architectural work is the destruction of the box.

The entrance to the theatre (plate 9b) contains a foyer on the ground level, but the lobby that opens into the house itself is above and leads the theatregoers into the house on three sides. The stage is designed to revolve and to move up and down. The scenery is placed on the stage on a lower level, then elevated to the house level and revolved as a more rapid change of scene is required.

9b

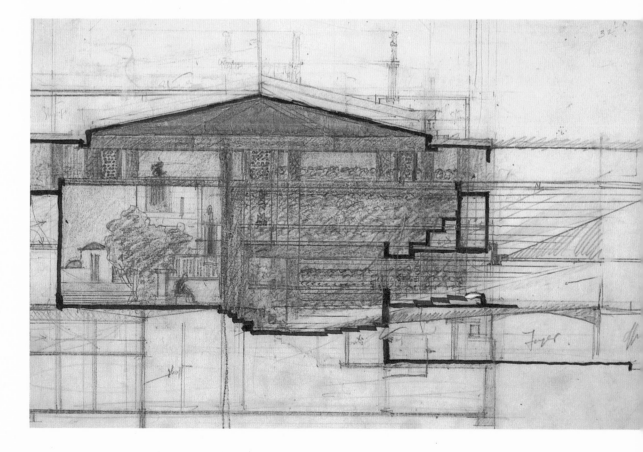

The project started in 1915, a year after Mr. Wright met Miss Barnsdall in Chicago where she was working in the first community theater in the United States. The smallish theatre was located in the Fine Arts Building on Michigan Avenue, a building in which other clients had built shops and galleries designed by him. When Miss Barnsdall moved to Hollywood to pursue her passionate interest in the theatre arts in California, she commissioned Mr. Wright to design not only a theatre but also to develop her large Olive Hill property into a theatre community, including a house for herself on the apex of the hill; two other residences, called A and B, for theatre staff; a long complex of shops and terraced houses; another separate residence called the Director's Residence; a theater for motion picture films; and the main theatre as shown here. The project went on for over five years. Eventually, she built the famous Hollyhock House and Residences A and B.

During the years from 1913 to 1921, Mr. Wright kept an office in Los Angeles as well as in Chicago, but he himself was traveling most of the time between the United States and Japan. These were the years during which the Imperial Hotel was in design stage and under construction. The innovative nature of the design demanded his presence at the building site for eight years. At the same time, he was working for Miss Barnsdall, and the time and space interjected between client and architect made frequently for a strained and difficult relationship. Miss Barnsdall was wealthy, impetuous, often demanding, imperious, but talented and aware of the genius of her architect. She could never settle in one place for very long, and the house that Mr. Wright built for her was the one residence where she spent the longest period of time somewhat "settled." Her restless spirit prevailed, and after a few years she gave it to the city of Los Angeles for a fine arts club.

The theatre project suffered likewise from the changeability of her character. At one point it was to seat 700 persons, then to seat 1500. Two models were made of two variations of the scheme, both lost now, except for their record in photographs. The dates on the drawings vary from 1915 to 1920. The sequence of the drawings is an almost impossible jigsaw puzzle because of the changes made over the years on the same sheets of paper. But the scheme as planned for a large house is nonetheless well recorded. The beauty and majesty of the sculptural concrete masses and the charming layout of the interiors with scenery and audience blended into one whole make this still one of the most remarkable theatre designs conceived at any point in time.

BARON GOTO HOUSE, TOKYO, JAPAN, 1921

On the small concept plan for this house is written, in Mr. Wright's handwriting, "Baron Goto, L.A. [Los Angeles], May 28, 1921." The identity of this client remains a mystery, but we do know that this was one of many residential commissions undertaken by Mr. Wright while he was at work on the Imperial Hotel. The proposed Goto house (plate 10) is one of the loveliest drawings in our collection, possessing a poetry and delicacy enhanced by the manner of its drawing. The drawing is small: the two elevations are on an 8 x 10 inch sheet of white art paper; the plans are on the reverse of the paper. The house as developed was to be large and spacious, obviously for a family of substantial means. The circumstances surrounding its commission and the reason it was never built remain unknown to this day.

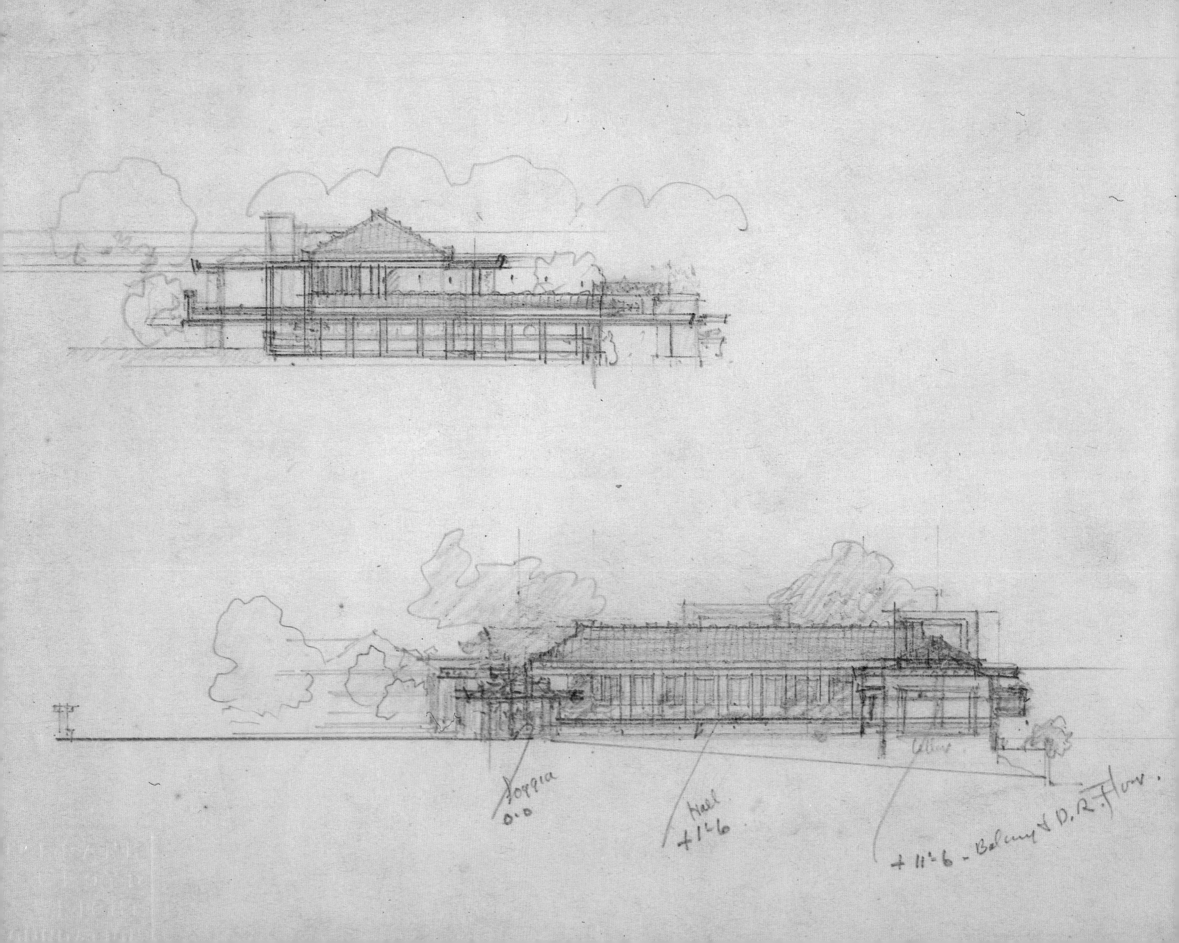

loggia
0:0

Hall
+1'-6

+11'-6 - Balcony & D.R. Floor

11a

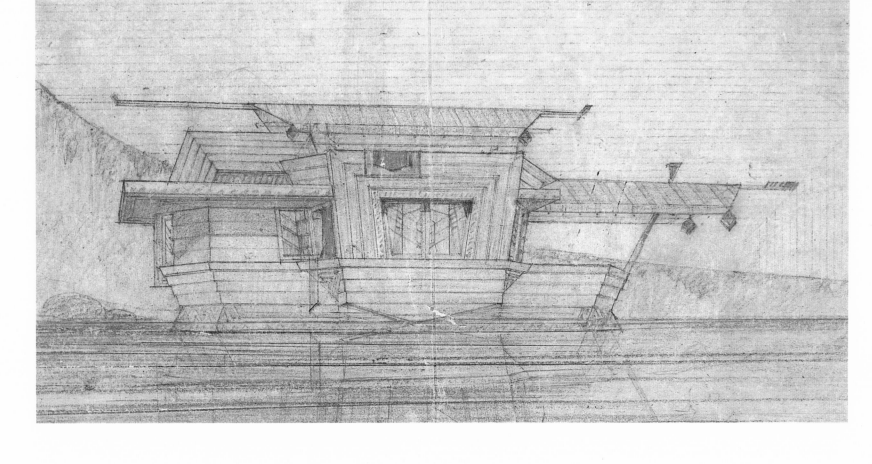

11b

LAKE TAHOE SUMMER COLONY, LAKE TAHOE, CALIFORNIA, 1922

The project for Lake Tahoe is a favorite among Frank Lloyd Wright scholars and enthusiasts. It represents an almost fantasy-like situation (plates 11a, 11b): cabins and lodges placed near the water's edge throughout a dense pine forest; additional lodges on the very water line itself; other cabins floating on the lake, linked together by a long dock or floating free as the case may be. The project also includes a main dining lodge and recreation area. The motif of the cabins and lodges derives from the forms of the surrounding pine trees. On some of the floating cabins the roof structure is supported by cables in such a way that the wind rushing through them "plays" on them like an aeolian harp.

Shortly after he made these delicate sketches, Mr. Wright discovered that the Los Angeles-based client had had no intention, from the very beginning, of ever building any of the designs. He wanted only to get the land promoted and therefore sold by using the architect's name. Mr. Wright tried to interest Aline Barnsdall in building the project, for she spent much time at Lake Tahoe and loved the region. But she rejected the idea.

The project, conceived in 1922, and as here illustrated, still presents a beautiful solution for vacation living in a spectacular landscape. And several times throughout Mr. Wright's work the Tahoe lodge theme reoccurred—for Piedmont Pines in 1938 and finally for a house for Richard Davis built in the fifties.

NATIONAL LIFE INSURANCE COMPANY, CHICAGO, ILLINOIS, 1924

Arthur M. Johnson, president of the National Life Insurance Company of Chicago, came to Frank Lloyd Wright in 1924 and commissioned an office building to be built near Water Tower Square in Chicago. Mr. Wright had begun plans for a cantilevered concrete, glass, and copper skyscraper in Los Angeles while working on the famous California concrete block houses after his return from Tokyo. His structural principle of employing the cantilever for safety had saved the Imperial Hotel from the ravages of the 1923 Kanto earthquake that had demolished most of Tokyo and Yokohama. Now Mr. Wright was eager to show that the same principle could be amplified to suit the skyscraper, making it more lightweight (most American skyscrapers at the time were greatly overweighted by stones stuck onto steel frames) and more stable, in keeping with the best use of twentieth-century materials and building methods.

Johnson was impressed by the survival of the Imperial Hotel and was willing to pay Mr. Wright a flat $20,000 fee to develop studies along the lines Mr. Wright had been thinking the year before in California. "Intensely interested in ideas, I believe," Mr. Wright wrote, "though himself not the kind of man inclined to build much. He seemed rather of the type called conservative, who, tempted, will sneak up behind an idea, pinch it in the behind, and turn and run. There is this type of man bred by our capitalistic system, not the captain, nor the broker or the banker, but a better sort, not quite contented with the commonplace, not quite courageous enough to take risks. I have met many such men."

The suspended walls of the proposed building (plate 12) are sheet copper and glass, suspended from the outer edges of cantilevered floor slabs. To avoid an excessive amount of glass on the outer surface of the building, about three-fourths of the skin of the building is sheet copper, properly insulated throughout. Within the building, a system of prefabrication makes it possible to locate and relocate all interior partitions according to the needs of the time, the space required for each occupant, and the changes required over the years. Because the building, inside and out, is an assemblage of unit-manufactured parts, construction on the site is relegated mostly to the concrete core and floor slabs. All the rest is made in the factory and then shipped to the building site and assembled. Here is the great cost-reducing factor: keeping the skilled craftsmen in the factory and off the building site. The shape and form of the building remains a twentieth-century product, like the beautiful and romantic concrete block houses in Los Angeles that Mr. Wright designed and built that same year.

He was able to show his sketches for the National Life Building to his *Lieber Meister*, Louis H. Sullivan, shortly before Sullivan's death in April, 1924. "I had faith it would come," Sullivan said as he looked over the drawings. "It is a work of great art. I knew what I was talking about all these years—you see? I could never have done this building myself, but I believe that, but for me, you could never have done it." "I know I should never have reached it but for what he [Sullivan] was and what he himself did," wrote Mr. Wright. "This design is dedicated to him."

Unfortunately, the design was never constructed. Arthur Johnson was indeed conservative, and though willing to grubstake ten or even twenty thousand dollars to create the idea, his interest stopped at that stage of the design. Having evoked plans for a remarkable building, he abandoned the scheme.

12

NORTH ELEVATION.

NAKOMA COUNTRY CLUB, MADISON, WISCONSIN, 1924

Whenever Frank Lloyd Wright designed projects for civic or public use for the Madison, Wisconsin, area they seemed destined to remain unbuilt. Paramount among these were the Monona Terrace, a large civic center (plates 22a, 22b, 61a, 61b) and the Nakoma Country Club (plate 13) designed in 1924.

The Nakoma project was to be built on the ceremonial campgrounds of the Winnebago Indians, and for this reason Mr. Wright conceived the structure as an abstraction of teepee forms, to honor and memorialize the area once sacred to the original inhabitants of the region. The first designs for the project used specially cast concrete blocks, but by the time the project went into the working drawing stage, the abundance of native limestone and the relatively low cost of stone masonry labor led the architect to change the basic material of the building. The roofs were board and shingles composed in certain areas in abstract designs, decorative features rising at various points along the elevation of the clubhouse. Inside, the rafters and beams followed the exterior lines and gave a lofty and dramatic height to the public rooms.

Having returned from Japan just two years before this project was created, Mr. Wright was excited by the idea of floor heating. This he saw first hand in the traditional Japanese homes, in a special room called the Korean room after the country where the idea originated. In the Korean room, floor-heated tiles supplied warm, radiant heat. Mr. Wright said that the only time he was ever warm enough in the winter during his time in Tokyo was either in the hot, steamy bath or sitting on the pleasantly heated floor of the Korean room.

He planned, in the Nakoma Country Club, for this floor heating to be achieved by means of iron pipes concealed under floor slabs or paving blocks. This type of heating he called gravity heat, because it worked on the principle of hot air rising and in turn forcing cold air down to the slab surface. Radiant heat, as such, can come from a radiator or a wall fixture of some sort and relies upon the air that passes by, whereas gravity heat works on the simplest of physical principles and is therefore self-sustaining. No artificial forcing of air is required; it simply rises as it becomes heated.

Mr. Wright contended that if one's feet and ankles are warm, the body is warm. But a person bundled up to the hilt will still feel cold from having cold feet and ankles. With floor heat, the body would require less heat and still be comfortable.

Although the Nakoma project had the support of several visionaries on the board of directors, the majority, conservative in outlook, voted it down. The neighborhood in which the club was to be built was one of primarily Tudor-type houses belonging to the above-average income citizens of Madison. They rebelled against the idea of a "modern" building constructed in their environs. The original committee that had commissioned Mr. Wright for the project had changed, and the more conservative new members had reservations about employing an architect whose personal life was at that time being exploited in the daily newspapers. Added together, all these objections defeated the project. Constructed in its stead was the average, run-of-the-mill Tudor clone that reassured the local citizenry.

Twelve years after Nakoma, however, in the S. C. Johnson and Son Administration Building, Mr. Wright's principle of floor heat was used with telling effect, and the following year it was used in the marvelously economical Jacobs house in Madison, Wisconsin.

Gordon Strong, a Chicago businessman, was attracted to the sense of engineering he saw in the work of Frank Lloyd Wright. Perhaps he can be likened to Chicagoan A. M. Johnson; both men were entrenched conservatives. His various letters to Mr. Wright and letters to others about the architect constantly reflect his disapproval of Mr. Wright's life-style at Taliesin. But at the same time they admit the genius of his sense of structure.

Whereas Johnson was looking for a feasible commercial building that would suit the realtor's needs and requirements of a city block (plate 12), Strong was anxious to develop a tourist facility in and around Sugarloaf Mountain, Maryland. He had begun to acquire property in the region and recognized that motor-touring was quickly becoming an American craze, along with hiking, horseback riding, and touring in general through beautiful scenic regions. The era of the state and national park was gaining more and more appeal. People wanted to get into their automobiles and visit the canyons, mountains, wilderness regions, and forests of the nation. Sugarloaf Mountain would give the touring public the "Automobile Objective," an accessible height to which the car could travel, overlooking the surrounding forests. The area would offer restaurants, cafes, shops, and other amenities designed to attract the traveling tourist.

Within the great Automobile Objective itself was designed a planetarium (plate 14): the outside view reveals the landscape of this earth; the inside view provides a landscape of the galaxies.

The project was abandoned shortly after it was designed. There was a heated and vituperative exchange of letters between architect and client. Strong objected that the structure was not appropriate to the site; Mr. Wright defended his work on the grounds that it was perfectly appropriate to both site and circumstance. Strong's objection was unfounded since appropriateness was the project's strongest feature.

Four years later, in 1929, Mr. Wright wrote to Strong:

Would you return to me the drawings made for the Automobile Objective on Sugar Loaf Mountain? It seems something of the kind is contemplated on the other side, in France, only in that case it is a museum. I hope you are well and that you and Mrs. Strong are happy in your lovely home at the foot of the mountain. We are here now for the summer, settled down at work, most of which is to be built in Arizona [San Marcos-in-the-Desert (plates 16a–16c)] but you will be glad to know including a tall building for New York City [St. Mark's Tower]. If ever you incline in this direction or are in the neighborhood, do come and see us and let us put you up. The skies are clearing for us and the future looks bright. Faithfully yours, FLLW.

The main theme of the proposed planetarium is undoubtedly the use of the spiral, a continual flowing of one level to the next. Years later, in the Guggenheim Museum that Mr. Wright designed in 1943, the spiral as a form for the structure within and outside finally came into being. Again in 1948 he employed the spiral, this time for the proposed Pittsburgh Point Park Civic Center (plates 43a–43d). In the Civic Center design the spiral becomes, as it did in the planetarium, a convenient automobile route, whereas in the Guggenheim Museum it is a pedestrian conveyance from the top level down to the ground level. In the V. C. Morris Shop in San Francisco, also designed in 1948, the spiral is a feature within the square frame of the shop's interior. The Morris Shop was a remodeling of a building already constructed in Maiden Lane, and the spiral ramp that encircles the interior open space is an access ramp, while in the Guggenheim Museum it is the essence of the interior. The building itself is one gigantic revolving spiral as a means of gaining better access from top to bottom without the encumbrance of steps, stairs, a change of static levels. In the Guggenheim, space becomes fully fluid in all dimensions. It is here in this building for Gordon Strong that the idea was born.

SKYSCRAPER REGULATION, 1926

In the mid 1920s, Frank Lloyd Wright made several trips to New York and became fully familiar with that particular metropolis for the first time around 1925–1926. He enjoyed going to New York, liked the multitude of events and cultural happenings that the city offered, and had many friends who lived and worked there, including Alexander Woolcott, Lewis Mumford, and editor Howard Myers. His younger sister, Maginel Barney, was a New Yorker, and he often stayed at her apartment in Greenwich Village.

As he traveled more and more throughout the United States, he saw other American cities following the New York trend, growing at a prodigious rate, expanding, sprawling, thrusting skyscrapers into the sky until all that was left on the ground below was a shadowed life in a man-made, darkened canyon. This condition prompted him to create a design solution for a section of city blocks anywhere, which he called "Skyscraper Regulation." In this scheme he showed that by means of careful attention to design in the first place, the tall building need not become the menace that it was distinctly becoming in New York.

Skyscraper Regulation (plates 15a, 15b) seeks to do just what its title implies: it regulates the height and direction of tall buildings so that one does not find a cavernous alley between walls of stone and concrete. The ground level is reserved for automobiles and smaller delivery trucks; larger trucking is kept underground, servicing the basement and storage areas of each city block. On the mezzanine level a sidewalk, in the nature, really, of a balcony, carries pedestrians across city blocks and over bridges, with gardens and planted areas interspersed to soften the sense of a world of steel, glass, and concrete. On the sixth-floor level, additional balcony-sidewalks gain ac-

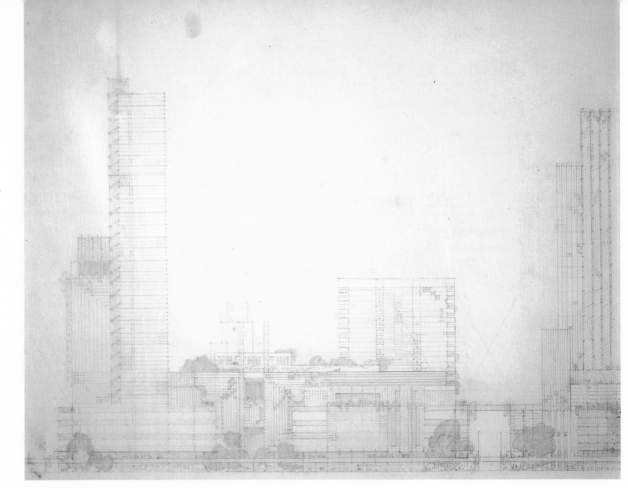

15b

cess around and across the grid plan. The sixth-floor levels of some of the buildings thus become garden parks with outdoor restaurants and rooftop recreation areas.

If one building rises as a thin slab running north and south, the building next to it is kept lower and rises on the east-west axis. The tops of the buildings are flat—no pretense at a cupola or gilded cage is made. One day his architect friend Raymond Hood asked him: "Frank, tell me, what do you do when you get to the top of the skyscraper? What sort of terminal or ending do you give it?" "Just cut it off, Ray," Mr. Wright replied. And this elevation of the Skyscraper Regulation shows just that application. A similar application showed up in later buildings such as the Rockefeller Center complex, where the structures simply ended flat on top, with the group of buildings placed so as to keep dark shadows and confining caverns to a minimum.

The actual skyscrapers, as Mr. Wright sketched them, consist of concrete cantilevered floor slabs with the outer layer, the "skin" of the building, made of glass and sheet metal. The glass is protected by the metal louvers or shades. Planting, generous as always in his work, softens the whole. Lightweight construction throughout was designed in lieu of the traditional masses of heavy masonry that characterized the major part of American skyscrapers at that time.

In this project, considerable attention has been paid to keeping the buildings on a human scale. The repetition of the mezzanine as a balcony on the sixth level reinforces this sense of scale and takes away that feeling of being lost within a dense concrete cavern that typifies most cities.

It would indeed be fascinating to see the project constructed in some burgeoning American city just as it was originally envisioned more than half a century ago.

15a

Alexander Chandler, trained as a veterinarian, founded the town that bears his name about twenty miles southeast of Phoenix. When he discovered that this Arizona region was ideal for growing cotton, especially a type of cotton needed in the manufacture of rubber tires, he branched out into large-scale land development. At the same time, he began to establish the town of Chandler as a tourist resort. He owned and ran the San Marcos Hotel in Chandler long before Phoenix became the central tourist region. Warm winter sunshine and dry air attracted vacationers from the Midwest and the East coast. Arizona was quickly becoming another Florida in its role of sunland and playland.

Frank Lloyd Wright was living in Phoenix during the winter of 1927 and 1928 while he was at work on the Arizona Biltmore Hotel. During that time, Dr. Chandler met with Mr. Wright to discuss a project for a new resort hotel, larger and more luxurious than anything Arizona had ever seen before, to be built outside of the town of Chandler on the south slopes of the South Mountain Range. The site was a splendid one for just such a hotel. There was a backdrop of crystalline rock formations rising above a wide mesa, approached by a deep arroyo, or wash, as these desert dry rivers and streams are called. Situated on the mesa of this mountain range the hotel would look south, ideal for the winter sun, across a protected valley and upon another, lower range of hills opposite. Nestled in between these two ranges, but with the sides to east and west open, the resort would be hidden from any highways, developing towns, or farmlands in the surrounding areas.

The approach to the structure was designed to make use of the gorgelike arroyo running up to the mountain's edge. In this way, the roadway could be concealed from sight, almost in the nature of a secret entrance. Across the mesa of this mountain range the hotel was to rise in a series of stepped-back terraces (plate 16a). Each room would have its own sunny terrace, plunge pool, and terrace-garden. Behind the rooms, all the corridors, closets, bathrooms, and storage areas were to be top-lit. Sunlight would pour in everywhere.

Late in the spring of 1928, Mr. and Mrs. Wright and their two children, Svetlana and Iovanna, left Phoenix and the work on the Arizona Biltmore Hotel and drove west to La Jolla, in California. The rebuilding of Taliesin, their home in Wisconsin, following the fire that demolished the living quarters in 1925, was nearing completion. However, Taliesin was still closed to them because of legal and financial problems. This project of a hotel commission for Dr. Chandler came as a blessing. It would free the Wrights from debt and permit them to return finally to their beloved home in southern Wisconsin. It was in La Jolla, where Dr. Chandler joined them, that Mr. Wright made his preliminary studies for the new hotel, to be called San Mar-

cos-in-the-Desert. These studies, rendered beautifully by Mr. Wright on off-white tracing paper in pencil and color pencils, are among the most treasured drawings in the Taliesin archive. They represent his very first thoughts on the project and reveal in delicate and precise lines the manner in which this work grew out of his imagination and onto paper.

The desert growth and desert environs were a particularly strong source of inspiration to Mr. Wright. The tall saguaro cactus, with its interior structure of slender reeds circling the center (thus conserving water in this area where water is as precious as diamonds), became, for him, a wonderful example of construction applicable to the methods of modern engineering and materials. His use of the concrete block system in the California houses of 1924 was inspired by this open-centered form. His concept of skyscrapers that are lightweight, flexible, and supported by a taproot foundation, like the saguaro, was another application of this structure in nature.

For San Marcos-in-the-Desert, the walls, ceilings, slabs, and terraces throughout all the spaces of the hotel are thin-walled, hollow-interior concrete blocks of varying patterns—some open and latticelike to let air and breezes pass through, others stamped with abstract geometric lines reflecting the character of the desert landscape.

The plan of the hotel and the manner in which the terraces are laid out conform entirely to the topographical lines of the site. The hotel virtually alights upon the desert like a great bird. No landfill is required, no taking away of the mountainside site is necessary. The roadway goes up and under the main front terrace; cars enter and turn around beneath this first terrace, shaded and protected. Stairways and elevators gain access to the level above with its lobby, called in the plan "living room," (plate 16b). Terraces front on the south and to the north for a view of the desert in one direction and of mountain splendor on the other. Mr. Wright and Dr. Chandler determined that this hotel would be no ordinary resort hotel. Rather, it was to be based on the idea of what today, some fifty years later, is called time-sharing. Families or individuals would own whatever space was required for their vacationing needs, and the rest of the year the rooms would be available on a regular, day-to-day basis for transient guests.

Above the lobby or living room is the dining room with its crystallike ceiling of glass, copper, and perforated concrete blocks. "We'll take those poor jaded New York millionaires out of their stuffy skyscraper towers in Manhattan and give them a life basked in sunshine and fresh air," Mr. Wright wrote.

On his return from La Jolla to Wisconsin, Mr. Wright stopped in Chandler to show the preliminary designs to his client (plates 16a–16c). He immediately liked them and told Mr. Wright he had been waiting for over ten years

16a

to develop that property. He knew of no architect capable of doing justice to the site on the desert except Frank Lloyd Wright. Dr. Chandler suggested they plan to start construction the following year (1929), and, in the meantime, would Mr. Wright prepare the working drawings.

The following winter Mr. and Mrs. Wright again arrived in Arizona, driving out of a Wisconsin blizzard. This time they brought with them not only their children but seven draftsmen as well to work on the San Marcos drawings. Rather than renting space in town for living and working, Mr. Wright designed and built the famous little desert camp outside of Chandler that was constructed of box cabins with canvas tops. The canvas flaps on the edges were dyed bright red, as suggested by the bloom of the desert ocotilla cactus that abounded in the area. When the camp opened, these touches of brilliant color inspired its name, Ocotilla.

Mr. Wright's architect son Lloyd came over from Los Angeles to work with them, and Paul Mueller, the builder of the Imperial Hotel, was called in to do the engineering. Ocotilla was located just beyond the first range of hills that would separate the new hotel site from the edge of the cultivated farm-

lands surrounding Chandler. The architect could thus work on his project within sight of the mesa that would soon house the building.

The working drawings completed, the concrete blocks designed and scheduled, the engineering finished, the project was ready to go ahead when the stock-market crash of October 1929 brought the work to a halt. Dr. Chandler was wiped out, as were the other investors who were to participate in the new hotel venture. Dr. Chandler was unable to pay Mr. Wright his architectural fees, and the drawings were rolled up and stored in the vault at Taliesin. Ocotilla was abandoned, and the next year neighboring Indians carted most of it away.

"I have found," Mr. Wright wrote, "that when a scheme develops beyond a normal pitch of excellence, the hand of fate strikes it down. The Japanese made a superstition of the circumstance. Purposefully they leave some imperfection somewhere to appease the jealousy of the gods. I neglected the precaution. San Marcos was not built. In the vault at Taliesin is this completely developed set of plans, every block scheduled as to quantity and place. These plans are one of our prize possessions."

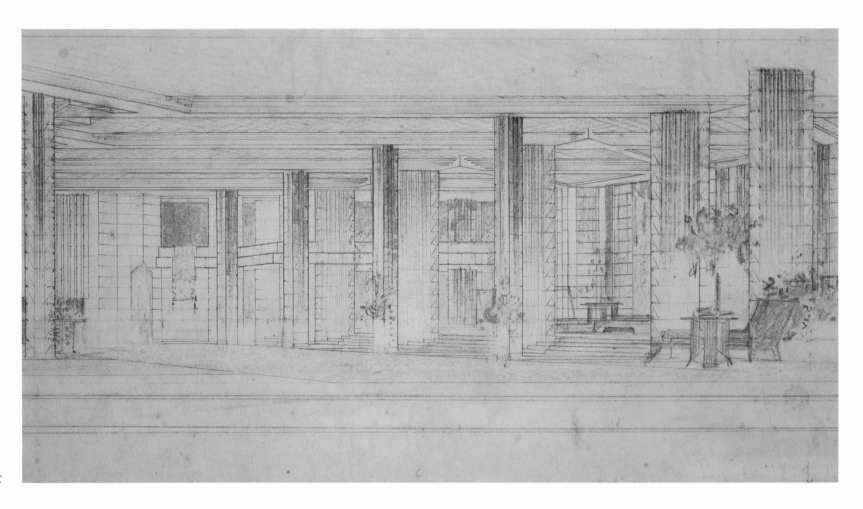

16c

Ten years later, Dr. Chandler asked Mr. Wright to design him another, but this time much smaller, resort hotel for the same site. Preliminary studies only were made for Little San Marcos, as it was called. But Dr. Chandler was never again to be in a financial position for such large-scale development.

In 1943, Dr. Chandler invited Mr. Wright to come to his cottage at the San Marcos Hotel for lunch and a trip out to some property he owned at Chandler Heights, some miles east of the town of Chandler. Kenn Lockhart, now one of the senior staff architects for the Taliesin Associated Architects, was then a recent member of the Taliesin Fellowship. Mr. Wright asked Kenn to drive him to Chandler. Following lunch, the three men drove out to the site upon which Dr. Chandler wanted to have Mr. Wright build him a house. The doctor was his usual vibrant and charming self. In his late eighties, he still possessed boundless energy and had what Mr. Wright called the most wonderful smile in the world. When they got out of the car, Dr. Chandler waved

his hand out across a prominent isolated hill and remarked excitedly, "Wouldn't this be an ideal site for something you could design?" Mr. Wright walked over the hill and continually remarked to the doctor about the beauty of the landscape with its unusual topography, always a challenge and an inspiration to him, and explained the residence that had instantly come into his mind. He was, in fact, designing the building right there in front of Chandler's eyes, and the doctor was immensely pleased, electrified by Mr. Wright's enthusiasm.

Later, when Mr. Wright and Kenn had left Dr. Chandler at his cottage on the grounds of the San Marcos Hotel, Kenn turned to Mr. Wright and asked: "Would Dr. Chandler really attempt to build such a large and extensive house?" "No," Mr. Wright replied, "I am afraid that he will not, but I believe that our visit with him and that walk over his property made for a very fine afternoon for the good Doctor, and I was glad to do it for him."

17a

CUDNEY AND YOUNG HOUSES, CHANDLER, ARIZONA, 1928

Two residences near the San Marcos-in-the-Desert Hotel were planned, one for the brothers Ralph and Wellington Cudney, the other for Owen D. Young. These men were New York financiers, part of Dr. Chandler's regular clientele who came each winter to Arizona from the cold, damp, wintry East Coast. They were part of the "poor millionaires" whom Mr. Wright wished to expose to the beauty of the Southwest desert in a setting that belonged to this zone. Until the designs for the San Marcos-in-the-Desert Hotel and these two houses were done, the usual style that prevailed in the environs of Phoenix was a watered-down version of Mission Spanish à la Los Angeles. Now with these buildings the desert could come alive with an atmosphere quickened by desert-oriented architecture. It was a classic case of what Mr. Wright meant when he stated that a beautiful landscape was made even more beautiful when a sympathetic and harmonious building was placed within it.

17b

Both houses, part of the overall hotel scheme, employ the concrete block construction technique that was to be featured in the main hotel. The Cudney house (plate 17a) was designed on the 30–60 degree triangular motif. Everything conforms to this pattern of the triangle as an inherent design system of desert growth. It was to be a large house, with a two-story living room and wings extending out along an arroyo behind the house as an accommodation for guests.

The Owen D. Young house (plate 17b), another large-scale residence, makes use of a most innovative variation on the regular grid system of the concrete blocks: they are turned on edge at 45 degrees. Many large rooms and ample guest facilities are provided for in this work, and the living room

is treated like a solarium, with sunlight pouring into the center from an open roof. These three works, including the hotel, were designed for winter living only, when the baking, dry warmth of the sunshine is a most appreciated element.

Along with the hotel, these projects were terminated before construction began because of the collapse of the stock market in October 1929. In fact, it was men like Cudney and Young who most suffered from the crash, because they were in the middle of the financial melee. Ralph Cudney once told Mrs. Wright during a visit to Phoenix in the winter of 1928, "My blood pressure and pulse rate, Olgivanna, go up and down right along with the daily rise and fall of the stock market!"

THE ROSENWALD SCHOOL, LA JOLLA, CALIFORNIA, 1929

Mr. Wright maintained that blacks had a keener perception and appreciation of color, geometry, pattern, and abstraction. He cited as an example their omnipresent use of decoration integral with whatever they built or made by hand: their native dwellings in Africa, their mode of dress, their body decorations, their jewelry, and their masks.

Twice in his career he was called upon to design projects specifically for blacks in America: in 1929 this small elementary school and in 1957 a large housing project for Whitefield, North Carolina. In both cases he made extensive use of color and ornament throughout the work.

His client and personal friend Darwin D. Martin was responsible for the school for the Rosenwald Foundation, designed for construction in La Jolla, California. Careful ex-amination of the details, of the decorative patterns edging the wood surfaces of the building, reveal his application of geometry and color (plate 18). He embellished with brilliantly colored enamel the wood grain and natural stains employed, giving the effect of a necklace of sparkling beads resting upon dark, velvet skin. The uses of acute angles make this building in many ways a forebear, a precursor, of the angular treatment he incor-porated ten years later in his own Arizona home, Taliesin West.

The Rosenwald School would have been a lovely youthful fantasy-place for children, an atmosphere permeated with joy in which they could learn. Unfortunately, as Mr. Wright's handwriting on the drawing's edge explained, the project was rejected on the grounds that it was not sufficiently "colonial."

18

Expositions and world's fairs are generally held in temporary buildings that are built on a huge scale and are theatrical in character, like vast stage settings out of doors. The buildings are quickly demolished once the fair is terminated; a great deal of expense and labor is thus thrown away. Two notable exceptions are the Crystal Palace erected by Joseph Paxton in 1851 in Hyde Park, London, and the tower that Gustave Eiffel built in Paris in 1899. The Crystal Palace was disassembled after the fair, moved to Sydenham, and reassembled; the Eiffel Tower remains to this day at the end of the Champs de Mars, beside the River Seine.

In Mr. Wright's view of architecture, a building should be built to last a long time, should be constructed with the intention of being a beautiful, viable, usable, practical structure in long-term service to mankind. All commissioned work that he himself designed and built was done so with this concern.

When Chicago was considering a world's fair in 1933 and decided to call it "A Century of Progress," some architects and other friends of Mr. Wright met in New York in 1931 to propose that Frank Lloyd Wright contribute a building to the fair and to protest his having been left out of the project altogether. Raymond Hood, Alexander Woolcott, and Lewis Mumford were among the friends with him at that New York meeting, urging him to join the team and participate in the fair. "Surely it was better to have one architect [himself] out of employment in such parlous times than the eight or ten already employed on the Fair?" he wrote. "Were I to come in they would go out because I could not work with them and would not work against them."

The architecture of the Chicago fair was to represent the century of progress that had taken place between 1833 and 1933. Gigantic achievements in the fields of structure, methods, and materials had indeed occurred over the past century. And those one hundred years saw communications, telephone, radio, electricity, literally hundreds of "progressions" from the century before. In the realm of building, steel, concrete, glass, and reinforced concrete were in use. A palette of extraordinary scope was in the hands of architects and engineers the world over as a result of these new materials and the new ways in which they might be used, combined, and developed. But outside of a few rare examples, and most of those done by engineers like John Roebling with his Brooklyn Bridge, few architects had taken advantage of these modern techniques. They used the materials, to be sure, but in ways and means that had not evolved since the post and beam constructions of the ancient Greeks.

During the New York meeting, realizing that he was not going to be chosen for work on the fair, Frank Lloyd Wright nonetheless "designed" three schemes while talking to the group, the New York Press included. His talk was in the nature of extemporaneous design-ideas, three in all, each one different, each a scheme for the entire fair: a skyscraper, a pontoon fair out on Lake Michigan, and, third, a series of suspended pavilions. Knowing full well that the project for the fair would not be his job, he nevertheless was eager to see his ideas crystallized and take form at least on paper.

He later described them in his autobiography as three progress fairs in one. Each project he described carefully and amply, beginning with the skyscraper version. "Why not, then, the Fair itself the apotheosis of the skyscraper? A mile high! . . . Instead of the old stage props of previous fairs, the same old miles of picture-buildings faked in cheap materials, wrapped around a lagoon, a fountain or theatrical waterfall in the middle—to be all eventually butchered to make Roman holiday—let there be, for once, a genuine modern construction to remain as a great memorial."

The mile-high skyscraper that he then designed for the fair, complete with five parking terraces and additional parking underground, was the seed out of which grew, in 1956, the Mile High Illinois (plates 64a, 64b).

Another scheme was proposed in which the fair would be on the lake surface "for a genuine holiday . . . a gay festival for the eyes. Why not a Pontoon Fair"?

Illustrated in plate 19 is the third scheme, a pylon and pavilion type of building project.

A weaving characteristic of this age of steel is tension. Accept from John Roebling his pioneer work—message of the Brooklyn Bridge. Build noble pylons, since the Fair commissioners seemed to like the word pylon—on the Lake Front five hundred feet apart each way until enough park, including threading waterways, had been covered to accommodate all exhibitors on the park level and in one balcony level surrounding the great enclosed area. This plastic-slung canopy to be anchored by steel cables to the outer series of appropriate pylons. . . . Thus make an architectural canopy more beautiful and more vast than any ever seen. The fabric should fall as a screen at the sides to close the space against weather . . . and, at least, the great pylons might remain always as lighting features of the Lake Front Park. Whereas the privatistic buildings faked in synthetic cardboard and painted would all have to be thrown away.

He planned for the foot traffic within the great canopies to be handled from level to level by means of escalators and on ground level by means of moving walkways.

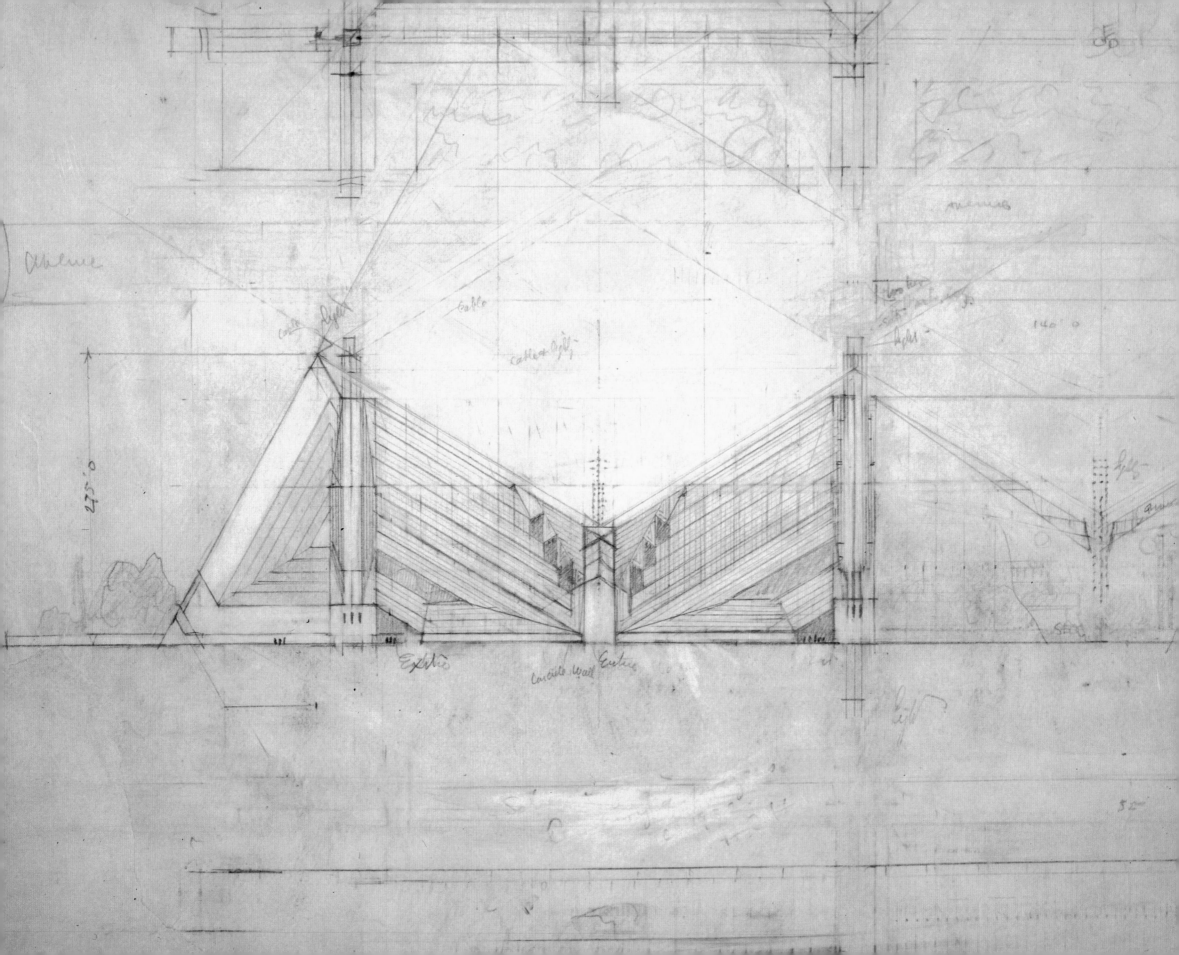

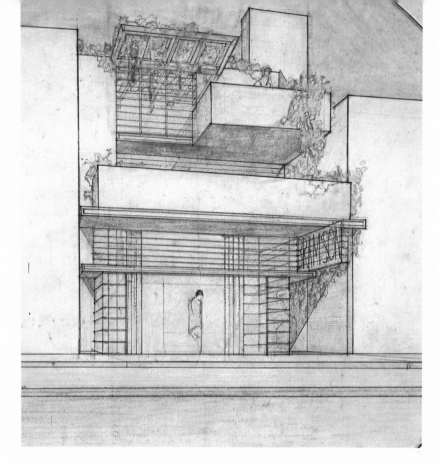

BRAMSON DRESS SHOP, OAK PARK, ILLINOIS, 1937

Henry Pebbles and his wife Grace, called Gracie by her close friends, ran a charming French restaurant in the fashionable Michigan Avenue section of Chicago called Le Petit Gourmet. They had both been longtime friends of Frank Lloyd Wright. Years before, Pebbles and O. B. Balch had built a shop designed by Mr. Wright in Oak Park for their interior decorating firm. Balch had also built a home designed by Mr. Wright.

It was the lovely and enthusiastic Gracie Pebbles who encouraged a Chicago suburb couturier, Leo Bramson, to have Mr. Wright design this shop and residence in downtown Oak Park (plate 20). The projecting balcony and concrete trellis above it constitute the two floors of an apartment for Bramson above the shop itself. Horizontal metal bars help to shield the glass areas and provide for the planting of vines that during the hot summer will let soft, filtered light into the shop. In the glare and bustle of a typical suburban downtown area, this screenlike effect of growing greenery would produce much desired relief. Although set between other buildings in a conventional city block, a sense of human scale perseveres. It is intimate amid its overbearing neighbors.

Years later, Frank Lloyd Wright designed for Nina Anderton the Anderton Court Shops, a series of three stories of shops built on Beverly Hills' Rodeo

Drive. Like the Bramson project, it possesses human scale, and the shock of seeing how much spaciousness can be achieved without undue height startles pedestrians who come upon the building.

"You can always make a friend out of your client," Mr. Wright often cautioned us, "I have many times in my life. But I think it unwise to make a client out of a friend. You will forever regret it, because should anything go wrong with the building regardless of whose fault it may be, your friend-client will accuse you of coercing him into something he didn't want in the first place."

The Bramson Dress Shop was urged onto one friend, Bramson, at the instigation of another, Gracie Pebbles. Through it all, the authority of the architect to stand by his design and his concept was lost, and the project was never built.

"MEMORIAL TO THE SOIL," CHAPEL FOR SOUTHERN WISCONSIN, 1937

The design for this chapel, intended for southern Wisconsin, was entitled by Mr. Wright "Memorial to the Soil." The particular area for which it was intended was the section of the state in which Mr. Wright was born, where he grew up, and where he built his home, Taliesin. It is a pastoral landscape rich in produce and noted for large dairy farms. Dense forests have been cut away to provide acreage for wheat, alfalfa, beans, and corn, indeed for all the field crops and garden vegetables imaginable.

Mr. Wright's boyhood was spent on the farm of his Uncle James. The architect's grandfather, Richard Lloyd-Jones, was a Welsh Unitarian minister who left Wales because he was regarded as a heretic and came to the United States with his wife Mary Lloyd and their ten children. Toward the middle of the nineteenth century, upon their arrival in the new land, they further migrated to Wisconsin and finally settled in the valley over which Taliesin now presides. The sons were farmers and preachers; the daughters, educators. It was Mr. Wright's mother, Anna Lloyd Wright, who first built Taliesin, designed by her architect son of whom she was fiercely proud. A strong person in her own right, she defended him, counseled him, and stood by him throughout his life up until her death in 1923. She loved architecture and in fact even before Mr. Wright was born she was determined that the child she was carrying would be a great architect. Accordingly, she hung illustrations of English cathedrals on the walls of the room he was to occupy as a child. Those aged prints, carefully preserved by Mr. Wright over the many years of his long lifetime and surviving the two major fires at Taliesin, are still in the archives of the Frank Lloyd Wright Foundation.

Anna Lloyd Wright saw the genius and imagination that was growing in her young son, and she saw his love for dreaming. She also firmly believed that the rigor, the hard work, the training, and the demands that life on a farm would impose upon him would be a necessary counterpart to those other creative and artistic tendencies that were evident so early in his life. It was a difficult decision for her to make, to give up her son and send him forty miles away to live with her brother. But she was willing to make the sacrifice on behalf of his development as a complete human being. Thus he was shorn of his long blond curls, with mother standing by crying all the while, and packed into a horse and buggy for the then long voyage to the Lloyd-Jones Valley. He adored his Uncle James and his Uncle Enos. They became great teachers for him, and he thrived on the farm, reveling in the hard work. He often quoted the phrase, "Adding tired to tired and then adding it all over again," with reference to these summers in the valley. His gratitude for his mother's decision remained with him always.

Thus, farming and a life close to the soil were strong factors in his life, instilled literally since childhood. They never left him. In his autobiography, the preludes that open each section of the book are reflections of this time in his life. When he established his residence at Taliesin at the suggestion of his mother, a farm unit was an essential part of the plan of work life. Horses, cows, steers, hogs, sheep, goats, along with field crops and vegetable gardens made Taliesin a nearly independent estate.

He was among the first to employ contour farming. The kitchen gardens were laid out in 1920 along the sloping banks of two hillsides, and he realized that if he were to preserve the valuable soil he must plow the slopes in terraces, as the Japanese and Chinese had done centuries before in Asia and the Incas had done in Peru. In 1920 this practice was indeed rare, and once in a while someone enrolled at the University of Wisconsin forty miles away would stop by at Taliesin and say: "My father remembers when he was a student in the agricultural college at the University and the professors would drive the students out to Taliesin on a Sunday afternoon to show them the contoured plowing."

The Memorial to the Soil Chapel was intended to be a dedication to the life of the pioneer farmer, growing out of a deep belief in the richness, almost sacredness, of the soil.

The plan (plate 21) is basically a square, chosen as a symbol of integrity and solidarity, oneness and unity. The entrance to the chapel is from the side, passing a large cast concrete sculptural abstraction. Inside, the walls of the chapel are ledges of packed earth, or berms, set into the ground, since the essence of the design was conceived as a memorial to the soil. A long, low window line continues around the top edge of the berm; a wooden overhang rises above this window band to meet the concrete slab roof above. Part of the berm wall ends in a perimeter garden of flowers at the window level. At the opposite side the wall extends down to floor level with a half-circle curve outside to hold a pool and fountain. Thus, from inside the chapel, a view at eye level on two sides reveals flowers and foliage planted on the berm. The

21

third wall of glass looks into the sunken fountain pool. Everything in the design, its forms, shapes, and human scale, emphasizes the ground, the soil.

When Mr. Wright was asked what was the role of sculpture or painting in this building, he replied: "My buildings *are* paintings and sculpture. But painting and sculpture that is architecture could enter where I am compelled to leave off for want of more highly specialized technique. To carry a building higher in its own realm is the rightful place of painting and sculpture, wherever architecture is concerned. Within this Memorial Chapel they are that and are so employed. Colored bas-relief heightens the memorial theme."

A committee in southern Wisconsin, called the Memorial to the Pioneers, originally commissioned the work. But the interpretation Mr. Wright gave to the memorial theme, as well as the design concept of the building itself, were so in advance of their own way of thinking that the project was abandoned. It went no farther than the preparation of preliminary drawings.

GLIN TERRACE

WILSON ST.

22a

MONONA TERRACE CIVIC CENTER (SCHEME ONE), MADISON, WISCONSIN, 1938

For so many American cities, the need for a so-called civic center was fulfilled by makeshifts—high school auditoriums, college or university field-houses and stadiums, state park areas, private halls and outdoor spaces, all to provide for concerts, exhibitions, expositions, shows, musicals, sports events, whatever may constitute a municipally sponsored event or occasion for public use. Without spaces or areas for these functions, a city would find itself off the circuit, and its citizens would miss the best and the finest of events that travel throughout the nation. Ideally, a city's civic center should provide space for many diverse functions, from athletics to art shows, from conventions to grand opera.

Madison, Wisconsin, was a makeshift civic center city, and being the state capitol as well as the location of a fine and growing university, it felt a strong need to move from the usual temporary arrangements with which it had long availed itself to something permanent, beautiful, practical, and centrally located under one roof with ample parking.

22b

In 1938, shortly after the first Jacobs house was built in Madison—an innovative solution for modest cost housing, a prototype that would spread across the Midwest and the East Coast—its contractor, P. B. Grove, and the noted landscape architect Franz Aust of the University of Wisconsin went to Taliesin to suggest that Mr. Wright make some sketches for a civic center for Madison. Grove had openly declared before the Jacobs house went into construction: "I'd give my right arm to build a building by Wright." Aust had been not only a landscape architect at the university but over the years a dedicated personal friend of Mr. Wright's.

Madison was constructed on the isthmus between two lakes, Mendota and Monona. The layout of the city was the typical Pierre L'Enfant plan, used to build the nation's capital. L'Enfant had all streets radiating out from central cores, like spokes from a wheel. In Madison's case the central core was the state capitol, at the narrow part of the land between the two lakes. Leading down from the capitol square and overlooking Lake Monona was an embankment called Olin Terrace. From this spot in the heart of the city Mr.

Wright proposed a civic center that would fan out over the lake below (plates 22a, 22b). It is composed of several levels, from the terrace above to the water below, and takes in land around the railroad tracks that ran directly below the embankment. Thus, the civic center would occupy no valuable land space in the city itself; it would be built literally in the air above the railroad tracks and the water's edge, a terraced park to the city and a great sheltering series of terraces becoming a marina to the lake.

An argument arose, however, among the authorities over the eventual location of the project. Some wanted to change the site from Lake Monona to Lake Mendota, on the other side of Madison. City officials also worried about costs and about the radical nature of the scheme; they finally decided to withhold the project until these issues could be resolved.

The Monona Terrace Civic Center of 1938 would have been just the structure that Madison needed and that its citizens wanted. But politics and conservatism prevailed. Madison lost the Monona Terrace project and finally had to settle on the costly revamping of an old movie house for a civic center.

JOHN NESBITT HOUSE, CARMEL, CALIFORNIA, 1940

The house (plate 23a) that Frank Lloyd Wright designed for radio personality and film producer John Nesbitt is one of the most lavish, most elegant houses he created during the last thirty years of his life. It is in a category with the house he designed for Harold McCormick in 1907 for Lake Forest. The materials were to be stone, wood, and semiprecious stones. The elegance of the scheme arises from the intricate way in which those materials are treated, always in keeping with their inherent nature, but with a detailing that turns the carpenter into a cabinetmaker, the stonemason into a jeweler.

The entrance to the house is through a covered gateway, with parking at the side in a four-car carport. A large, sixteen-foot-diameter circular pool called the Master Pool stands to the left of the doorway that leads into the loggia. From this fountain pool, other pools and fountains are supplied with water. The loggia is a spacious reception area looking into an enclosed garden space open to the roof three stories above but protected by skylights against wind and rain. The main dining area is found at the left of the interior garden, while directly facing out to the sea are long plates of full-length glass set well back under a large overhang. On this ground level are kitchen facilities, storerooms, wine rooms, silver, glass, and china rooms. A breakfast room adjacent to the main dining room also looks out to the sea.

23b

Access to the main living area is by means of a hanging staircase in the centrally located enclosed garden. This dual living area is called, on the plans, Great Hall (plate 23b) and Sea Lounge. One flows into the other, the Great Hall with a high ceiling, the Sea Lounge lower, broader, with emphasis on the lookout to the ocean beyond. These two rooms, really treated as one but separated by a row of stone columns, offer five thousand square feet for the extensive amount of entertaining required by Mr. and Mrs. Nesbitt. Their own private bedrooms, dressing rooms, studies, and gallery are located on this same level, above the dining and food preparation area. From the ground-level loggia to the ceiling of the Great Hall and Sea Lounge rise sculptured stone columns. But each column is cut off two feet short of the ceiling and topped with a sixteen-inch-diameter sphere lighted from within the top of the column. Each of the eight spheres is made of semiprecious stones: malachite, lapis lazuli, onyx, porphyry, chalcedony, jasper, jade, and rose quartz.

A covered boardwalk follows the lot line around the entire property and connects guest houses, servants quarters, conservatory, and greenhouse to the main building. From the Master Pool at the entrance, water follows a course to the next pool in the enclosed garden. Alongside this second fountain pool rises the hanging stairs, flanked by one of the sculptured columns coming out of the pool to the skylight above. The other pools are outside the plate glass windows of the entry loggia. They are grouped as a cluster of large circles at different levels, stepping down the slope from the house to the seashore's edge below.

Although the house appears to be simple lapped-board wood throughout, the boards are perforated in places with geometric patterns containing concealed lighting. No direct lighting exists anywhere within the house. All sources of light are built-in, the glowing illumination coming from different indirect sources cut into the wood paneling, the ceiling boards, the deck boards, and the upper areas of the walls. Daylight in places comes into the rooms in the same fashion, through intricately designed and carved openings in the stained and waxed cypress.

Elegance is apparent at every turn. Massive fireplaces plus small, intimate ones bring strong masonry accents to an otherwise all-wood house. Planting in the central enclosed gardens makes an indoor forest or glen where a person enters the building. Once inside the visitor suddenly feels the out of doors and looks beyond to the great seascape, blocked off until this moment. But here the ocean is seen only in glimpses between stone columns and rich planting. Once the stairway is mounted and a 180-degree turn is made, the Sea Lounge provides the true drama of this plan—the ever-changing ocean directly out front, below, literally at one's feet.

The intervention of the Second World War abruptly stopped the construction of the house whose only memento is a beautiful and complete set of working drawings.

CONNECTICUT AVENUE ELEVATION

SCALE 1"

CRYSTAL HEIGHTS, WASHINGTON, D.C., 1940

In October 1940, speaking on the design for a large project to be built in Washington, D.C., on a radio interview sponsored by the Madison Capital Times, Frank Lloyd Wright said, "As to Crystal City, Washington, D.C., doesn't the real significance of that Washington work lie in the fact that while most of the country has lost faith in democracy and turns toward armament

24a

large scale development project approximately heart of Washington, D.C. Kindly wire me collect, Gladstone Hotel."

"Will be here and glad to see you," Mr. Wright immediately replied. Following the meeting at Taliesin, Thurman wrote to confirm what they had discussed, explaining that he had purchased a tract of land known as the Dean Estates, sometimes called Temple Heights. Thurman was an enthusiastic young man, extremely likeable and charged with a sense of vision.

His proposal called for a hotel of one thousand rooms, plus residential apartments along with shops, parking garages, and a theatre to seat one thousand persons. By the end of August, the scheme was fully developed by Mr. Wright, conceived and designed in a remarkably short period of time (plate 24a). The basic concept for the taller buildings was a further outgrowth of St. Mark's Tower, which he had designed ten years earlier for William Norman Guthrie in New York City. St. Mark's Tower was a tall shaft of cantilevered slabs supported by a central core that contained elevators, stairs, and utilities. The exterior walls were screens of copper and glass, the glass areas shielded by louvers of copper.

Along with the preliminary drawings Mr. Wright sent the following description of the project:

My dear Roy Thurman:

Herewith a pan-out of the buildings I've planned for you at Washington. I think it will astonish you. I am like the lady who played the piano for her own "amazement." Certainly the whole thing shapes up in remarkably productive and beautiful form. But I can't see more than seven and a half million in it—at that. I am mortified to have fallen short of the ten or twelve you mentioned. Perhaps my imagination is less active than it might be.

The scheme for the Hotel is ideal from a practical standpoint, as any portion of it may be apartments of any one of the classes you mentioned. There is no break between Hotel and Apartment. The scheme for the Hotel proper is greater in scope and beauty than any in the world. The whole thing should be worked out in white marble, verdigris-bronze and crystal, and show up the Capitol for a fallen dumpling and Washington hotels as insufferable. And this is to suggest that you change Temple Heights to CRYSTAL HEIGHTS because of the crystalline character of the whole edifice. It will be an iridescent fabric with every surface showing of the finest quality. There are no accommodations in Washington or any other city so luxurious and spacious in effect. Crystal is the word when you see the buildings.

I have assumed that you wanted the last word which is also the first word in all this and we have it—the apotheosis of GLASS.

The floor surfaces which are extensive inside and outside will receive great attention—be of white marble with bronze shallow bas-relief inlays at appropriate places emphasizing the great spaciousness in bright light of the whole structure. The gardens and terraces all contribute to this effect too. I've managed to save the better part of the oaks. The Dining Room Banquet Hall and all Private Support Rooms are all sunlit overlooking garden terraces—gleaming crystal palaces [plate 24b]. Versailles is no more.

and war, private enterprise with calm assurance in the future of our country can invade the very center of alarum and disturbance to begin the greatest building of modern times?"

The project had been set in motion in August of that same year when Mr. Wright received a telegram from Roy S. Thurman stating, "I expect to be in Milwaukee within next few days and would appreciate hearing whether it would be convenient to visit you for purpose of discussing most unusual

But before I show this new "Arabian Nights Entertainment" to you I want double assurance doubly sure that no "Lessee" is to come in on this to tell me how to spoil it in any or every particular.

You neglected to give me that particular in the written memo you sent. Although you promised it enthusiastically, it might pass beyond your control.

We have here a great demonstration of the desirability of genuine organic building as against the building that curses Washington so clear, it seems to me, that even "money" can see and appreciate it. But maybe money is really "blind as a bat" unless a man like you can be its eyes and see.

I have assumed that you wanted to make a clean sweep of the success of Crystal Heights—and I am proceeding accordingly with a thoroughbred.

After all, no half-way measures, or men either, are ever greatly successful. This calls for protective administration of what it has to give to Washington, and that ought to mean to the world.

The layout follows on next pages:

CRYSTAL HEIGHTS: WASHINGTON D C
MATERIALS: White marble slabs. Bronze and Crystal.
HOTEL: (Rooms—glass two sides of ¾ of all rooms or Crystal Apartments). All rooms interchangeable as large-singles or two room or single room apartments.

124 medium size rooms and baths in 3 upper towers.
588 medium size rooms and baths in 7 stories
382 large rooms with baths in 7 stories
28 large rooms with baths in 7 stories of entrance towers
56 medium rooms with bath in 7 stories of entrance towers
32 medium singles and baths in 2 lower south terraces
20 medium singles and baths in 2 lower north terraces
1230 rooms with bath.
410 large rooms with bonafide fireplaces and baths—glass two sides
820 medium size rooms and baths

SEPARATE APARTMENTS:

32 studio apartments (3 rooms and 2 baths)
10 attic studio apartments between stacks
32 large single room apartments
64 medium single bachelor apartments

CRYSTAL BANQUET HALL: Seating 1000 at table and one row tables in balcony.
Twelve private Supper Rooms—approximately 16' × 20'.
Terraced main Crystal Dining Room joining two sides of central oak garden seating 1000 around garden.
(Note: direct access to kitchen departments for all).

OAK TREE GARDENS: Flower terraces and fountains 90,000 sq.ft. Oak Park behind towers 564' × 64'.
SHOPS:

28 South Terrace by Cinema
44 Connecticut Avenue Terraces
72 Shops

(Approximately 24' × 100')
Parking space on rear drive for all.

PARKING SPACE:

South Terraces:	100,000 sq.ft.
Connecticut Stores	10,000 " "
Theatre	12,000 " "
Hotel parking and	
Banquet Hall	120,000 sq.ft.
	242,000 " "

200 sq.ft. to a car   1400 cars
(Note: a procession of cars seven miles long could turn in on the parking shelves)

CRYSTAL BAR
CRYSTAL COCKTAIL LOUNGE. 30 × 400' CRYSTAL ALLEY AND LOBBY (100 × 75')(for tea and promenade)
9 BOWLING ALLEYS under terrace Connecticut Avenue
UNIQUE CINEMA (Loge Seating) 1100: large foyer connected with flower, toy and candy shops. All seats on lower levels.
GALLERY AND MUSEUM on Connecticut Avenue between Avenue and Hotel Entrance.   30,000 sq.ft. (or spacious Art Store).
ENTRANCE TUNNEL (taxicab parking) 22 waiting cabs not interfering with traffic in or out.
On this tunnel Baggage rooms and storage.
Under Banquet Hall are main Kitchen Departments and Refrigeration.
Under Lobby: Barber Shops—Turkish Baths—Beauty Parlors.

NOTES:
Private Supper Rooms suitable for small lecture rooms. Banquet Hall suitable for concert Hall. Crystal Alley or promenade suitable for tea or lounging.
Terraces so continued that immediate surroundings are all blotted out so that all upper terraces and most room exposures open to the South—view of Washington Monument and Potomac.

Frank Lloyd Wright
Taliesin
Spring Green
Wisconsin
August 27th, 1940

Throughout the summer and fall the letters continued between Mr. Wright and his client as the project was refined, estimated, and planned down to each engineering detail. But by January of the following year, the beautiful Crystal Heights was defeated by a zoning law that forbade any tower higher than 110 feet, as well as by various civic groups in Washington who were horrified to see the nation's capital on the verge of building a modern building. It was finally killed off by the solemn conclusion that "any edifice that is not Greek, nor at least Colonial, is unfit for the Nation's capital." Mediocrity won. The plans were returned to Taliesin and stored away.

"EAGLEFEATHER," ARCH OBOLER HOUSE, MALIBU, CALIFORNIA, 1940

Arch Oboler was one of Mr. Wright's most interesting, and certainly most eccentric, clients. A radio scriptwriter and film maker, he was responsible for such programs as "Lights Out" and "Inner Sanctum" and for the development of 3-D motion pictures. He first came to Mr. Wright in 1940 for a house on a small mountain in Malibu, several miles from the sea up in the hills with a distant view of the ocean. Eaglefeather (plate 25) was the house Mr. Wright designed for him, with its projecting balcony soaring out to the distant seashore. Being a residence for a film maker, the house naturally contains a projection room, film vault, and provisions for cinema viewing.

From 1940 to 1957, Oboler was a continual client. Some of his projects were built; others, such as this house, were not. Oboler began with a gatehouse on his land and then extended that with a nursery wing for his growing family. His wife, Eleanor, who dressed almost exclusively in brightly colored gingham pinafores, appeared for all the world like a character from Lewis Carroll. For her, Mr. Wright designed and built Eleanor's Retreat, a small mountain cottage up the hill slope from the gatehouse.

Oboler's gatehouse became the setting for his motion picture *Five*, a story involving five persons left in the world following a nuclear holocaust who migrated from desolated Los Angeles to this setting in the high mountains.

Oboler's fortunes ebbed and flowed with his various film-making projects, but his enthusiasm was without end. When he was building another addition to the gatehouse he wanted stones of all varieties and journeyed around the country in a van collecting them, even coming to Taliesin West for some of the brightly colored stones in the region of Maricopa Mesa. Sometimes his enthusiasm and his initiative got in the way of the instructions from his architect. The letters between them are often pointed and barbed, with Mr. Wright scolding him mercilessly for interfering with the integrity of his design in his, Oboler's, eagerness to get it built. But Mr. Wright was always fond of him and enjoyed his visits to Taliesin.

The correspondence between Frank Lloyd Wright and Arch Oboler would fill a volume in its own right. One telegram from Oboler came to Mr. Wright at the time he was making the working drawings for Eaglefeather. "Still waiting for plans you promised three weeks ago. Should I plan house on cliff or in heaven? Arch Oboler." "Have been busy saving you from living in Hell. Ready for builder to come at once. FLLW."

On one of his visits to Taliesin West, early in their relationship, Oboler brought a small portable radio that fascinated Mrs. Wright. Radios up to that time were rather bulky and heavy, clumsy at best. Here was one that was small, had a clear tone, and was easy to carry around. He set the radio down on a table in front of Mrs. Wright, turned it on, and let her play it, moving from station to station. "It is absolutely remarkable, Mr. Oboler," she said. "I can't believe that such lovely tone can come from such a small thing. And to think it can be carried from room to room without having to plug it in. It is a miracle!" He sat with a small-boy, impish look on his face, held his finger to his lips as if to signify, "Don't say a word to anybody," smiled broadly and said, "It's yours!"

Eaglefeather was an ideal design for a person of Oboler's temperament: a creative writer who needed on one hand a quiet, reposeful, and inspiring place to work and on the other hand a comfortable home for his family and for the entertainment of friends. At the entrance level, riding the crest of a hill-ridge, is a swimming pool with dressing-room facilities adjacent. Tucked into the core of the main masonry mass that rises and supports the house is a room called Secret Retreat, where Oboler could lock himself in and write, with a spectacular view out under the main projecting balcony to practically all of southern California stretched beneath him.

Above, a large living space allows each room to have access to a balcony terrace; an open well borders the stairway with a top light above it. Desert masonry, composed of rocks placed in wooden forms and held in place with poured concrete, is the main stabilizing material for the house. The other material was planned to be redwood or cypress boards, used in the typical, lapped-board parapet type of design that so characterizes one phase of Mr. Wright's work.

While preparing to build Eaglefeather, Oboler decided first to build something smaller on that same property. Perhaps he feared actually plunging into a major construction project. Many clients did. In Oboler's case, he asked Mr. Wright to design the gatehouse and retreat described above the year after the Eaglefeather working drawings were finished. Both of those were built, and Mr. and Mrs. Oboler took up permanent residence in them, with subsequent additions and extensions of the gatehouse until it became in its own right a major building. Eaglefeather was indefinitely postponed, the victim of delays and procrastination, until it was clear that Oboler had lost interest in it.

FRANKLIN WATKINS STUDIO-RESIDENCE, BARNEGAT, NEW JERSEY, 1940

Franklin Watkins was a successful American painter. His family was from the exclusive Main Line area just outside of Philadelphia. Watkins, a cultivated person who easily reflected his background, owned beachside property in Barnegat, New Jersey, overlooking the Atlantic Ocean. Not a cliff-type piece of land, it was, instead, a rolling panorama of sand dunes.

The studio-residence that Frank Lloyd Wright designed for him in 1940 was meant to nestle into the dunes and look out to the ocean beyond (plate 26). The lower level contains a covered carport to protect the vehicles against salt spray. Also on this level is a small kitchen and dining area, as well as a bedroom and bath. A stairwell at the entry connects to the upper level, which is given over entirely to the studio with its tall windows, protective overhang, and balconies.

The simplicity of the plan is almost spartan. Watkins, who lived alone, devoted most his time to his painting; everything else took second place. Living, dining, and sleeping provisions in this design are minimal. But the studio on the second level is planned on a large scale. It is obviously the main feature of the design. The house's overall character gives it the appearance of charging across the dunes toward the Atlantic.

The grammar of the house is wood construction, totally carpenter's work, as the perspective shows and as the final working drawings further testify. When the drawings were finished, Mr. Wright sent them to the client along with this letter of explanation about the construction details of the project:

My dear Franklin Watkins:

Sorry I've neglected to send you this sooner but have expected to be in your neighborhood soon ever since talking with you in New York. Will certainly be in Philadelphia September 19th for the University of Pennsylvania Conference.

Meantime, this recipe.

A carload (board feet—better get this from your builder so he will be responsible) of rough sawed but accurately sized cypress or red-wood boards, well air dried or if this cannot be had, then, kiln dried. No machinery other than sizing with the . . . [illegible] needed because they all go on with a simple overlap and are screwed to each other at the unit lines up and down as well as cross-wise.

Some months after they are screwed up and the sun has had a chance to beat down on them in place, run a ½" Vulcatex bead: (A.C. Horn Co., Long Island City, N.Y.) on each joint outside and inside, put on with the mastic gun made and sold for the purpose. Should any defects show in the lumber like cracks or knots or none of all this, just take them out and insert others.

The roof boards are the same as the other boards except for the milled gutter battens carrying the water off and are to be treated the same in every way. The screws in this case to come up from the underside to avoid making holes in the water shed.

To stay the walls during construction, temporary horses of 2 × 4s can be used or any other expedient that may occur to your builder.

The inside brackets reaching from just about the floor to the ceiling could be used if temporarily set up in place.

Or, the board roof could be constructed entirely first on temporary horses, then the inside brackets be fastened to them like studs and the outside walls put on over them.

There is really no structural difficulty in getting the boards together so far as I can see.

It is important, however, to get good dry lumber.

The integrity of the full inch rough sawed board is the basis for the structural integrity of your building.

Incidentally, you should use cadmium plated screws with an electrical screwdriver that sends them in like driving a nail only easier and quicker. These screws will not stain the wood.

After the structure has been standing a few months (before beading with the mastic) these screws can all be gone over and tightened up. In this way you will have a mono-material building, same inside as outside and fairly good protection. You have your big fireplaces for emergencies.

I guess I would better leave the rest (questions I can't just now foresee) to be answered as they come up.

Any good (not too "EXPERT") carpenter can get the boards together if he will study the details carefully enough. The details are fairly complete. But we will make more if you need them. I hope you get going soon. And going should be fun?

Sincerely,

Frank Lloyd Wright

August 6, 1940

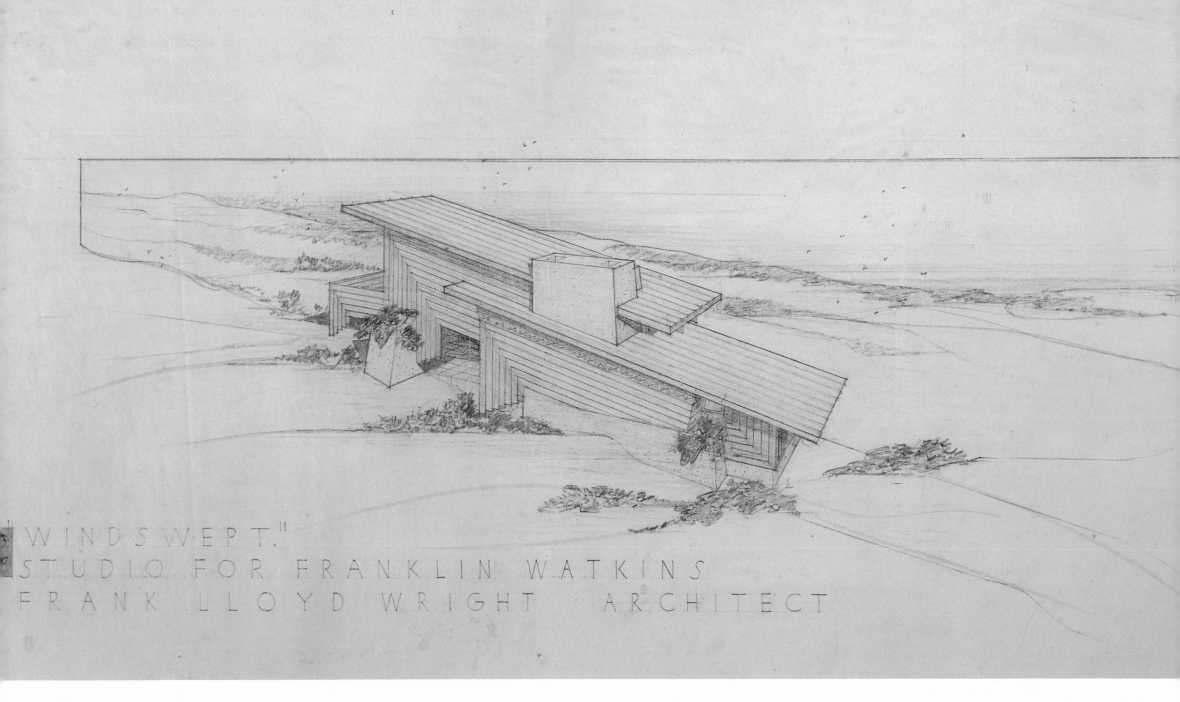

"WINDSWEPT."
STUDIO FOR FRANKLIN WATKINS
FRANK LLOYD WRIGHT ARCHITECT

27a

COOPERATIVE FARMSTEADS, DETROIT, MICHIGAN, 1942

A group of auto workers, teachers, and other professionals in Detroit formed in the late thirties a cooperative organization for the purpose of buying land in the country and starting construction on a group of moderately priced houses for themselves and their families. Eventually, they purchased a 160-acre farm to begin their venture. At about this time, early in 1941, Taliesin apprentice Aaron Green was in the Detroit area. He met with the cooperative in Detroit and was impressed by their idealism in trying to break out of the ordinary and establish something new. Besides helping to build each others' homes, they also planned to raise crops for their own consumption and for a small but welcome additional revenue. Aaron believed that what they planned to do would fit in perfectly with Mr. Wright's ideas about decentralization, moderate-cost housing, and leaving the overcrowded city for the country where one could live in harmony with the surrounding landscape. Prompted by Aaron's encouragement, some of their representatives came to Taliesin to discuss their project with Mr. Wright.

Mr. Wright was at this time interested in experimenting with rammed earth construction, and this seemed a good place to start. As soon as the drawings for the project were under way, Aaron returned to Detroit and stayed on to help the group get started. They purchased bulldozers, tractors, and other building equipment and drew lots to see which family's house would be the first to be constructed. Rammed earth walls were formed and a protective roof covering was begun, but the Second World War intervened. Many of the would-be dwellers were conscripted for one cause or another, either back to Detroit for defense work or into the armed services. Aaron himself enlisted in the air force, and while waiting to join was drafted by the army. Trying to explain that he was already in the armed services proved fruitless, and he was jailed until the air force came to the rescue. With the loss of the labor force the project dwindled. The winter snows came and the incomplete berm walls of the prototype model were washed out. The coop houses for Detroit thus became another war fatality.

But the project, as designed in 1942 (plates 27a, 27b), was the pioneer of rammed earth and earth berm construction. The walls, or earth berms, were to be treated with plaster on the inside surfaces, the earth berms outside planted with a variegated pattern of grasses and mosses. The wide overhang would protect the outside berms. A central section of the plan retains the berm behind stepped wall masses in order that full-length glass doors may give access to the ground level. Windows along the tops of the earth berm walls flood the interior with light, yet are also protected by the eaves.

The main problem of any type of rammed earth construction, including adobe construction, is how to guard against the capillary action set off where a rammed earth wall makes contact with ground soil. In other words, the rammed earth wall tends to draw moisture out of the ground and pull it up into the building unless a barrier or shield between the wall and the ground is erected. When the Indians of the Southwest built with adobe in and around New Mexico, they were aware of the same problem and were careful to construct a foundation wall of stone to protect the adobe wall rising on it. Mr. Wright also foresaw the problem and took the necessary steps to overcome it. Had he had the plastics, coatings, and waterproofing substances that exist today but were unavailable then, the rammed earth method might have been used far more extensively than it has been.

The Cloverleaf housing project for defense plant workers in Pittsfield, Massachusetts, was offered to Frank Lloyd Wright in 1942. He had designed and built a quadruple housing scheme, Sun Top Homes, some years before for Otto Mallery near Philadelphia. It was an ingenious solution to housing, placing four families in one structure but in such a way that each felt its own privacy totally maintained. In fact, one of the units in the Sun Top Homes once caught fire, and the fire department came in the middle of the night and extinguished the blaze while the other three families slept soundly through the entire experience.

Mr. Wright himself wrote this account of the Pittsfield project, his first commission from the United States government:

A long distance call, from housing administrator Clark Foreman in Washington, said, "I don't see your name anywhere on our roster. Why don't you contribute something?" "I'd like to," I said, "but I've never been asked."

"Well, I guess I understand that oversight, but I think we ought to end it. Will you do a project for us?" I said I would. Finally, 100 houses in Pittsfield, Massachusetts were told off to me and after I visited the site, I went to work. When the plans were nearly finished, a telegram came telling me to stop. It seems Mr. Foreman had been superseded by another. But since the project was nearly completed, I was authorized to finish it.

In Washington all were quite generally delighted with it. Some doubts as to detail had to be resolved. But sometime later word reached me that the local architects of Massachusetts had taken the matter up with their Congressmen and that only local architects as provided for in a statute covering the matter would be allowed to handle the project.

Although the government offered to buy what I had done, I declined to sell it because I would have no positive control over execution and so this project is still one of the best shots in our locker. In this scheme, standardization is no barrier to the quality of infinite variety to be observed in nature.

No entrance to any dwelling in the group is beside any other entrance to another dwelling. So far as any individual can know, the entire group is his home [plate 28b]. He is entirely unaware of the activities of his neighbors. There is no looking from front windows to backyards: all the private functions of family life are here independent of those of any other family. Playgrounds for the children, called sun decks, are small roof gardens placed where the mother of the family has direct supervision over hers. Family processes are conveniently centralized on the mezzanine next the master bedroom and bath, where the mistress of the house can turn a pancake with one hand while chucking the baby into a bath with the other, father meantime sitting at his dinner, lord of it all, daughter meantime having the privacy of the front room below for the entertainment of her friends [plate 28a].

"CLOVERLEAF"
TYPICAL LIVING-ROOM
LOOKING IN THROUGH WINDOWS

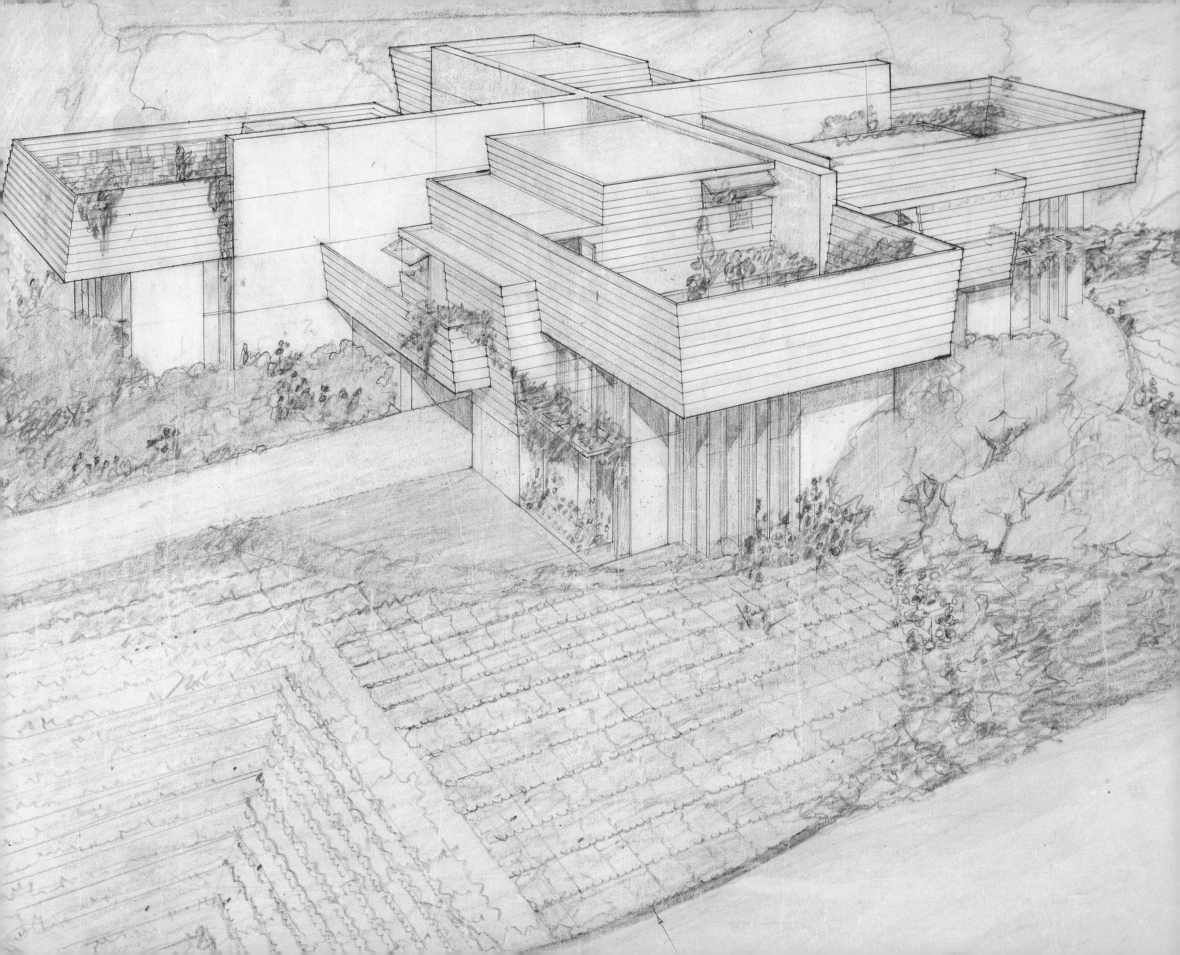

Dr. Ludd M. Spivey was the founder and president of Florida Southern College. In the spring of 1938, he attended a special fund-raising meeting with various members of his faculty and staff. He outlined the future of his then-small college, as he saw it. He had been acquiring buildings on a lakeshore site in Lakeland, Florida, and converting them to house his staff, faculty, and students, along with the facilities required by the college for its educational purposes.

At a certain point in his discussion of the college's future, one of his staff interrupted him with the suggestion: "Since you are dreaming such dreams for the future of this college, why not build a new campus altogether designed by a man of vision"? "And who would you suggest?" Dr. Spivey replied. "Frank Lloyd Wright" was the instant answer. The idea took root in Dr. Spivey's imagination, and he sent the following wire to Mr. Wright on April 11, 1938: "Frank Lloyd Wright, Jokake Inn, Arizona, Desire conference with you concerning plans for great education temple in Florida STOP Wire collect when and where I can see you. LUDD M. SPIVEY President Florida Southern College Lakeland, Florida." Mr. Wright replied: "Can you come to Taliesin Spring Green Wisconsin for conference." "Arriving there April 20th. LUDD M. SPIVEY." The meeting occurred on April 21 at Taliesin and began a relationship that quickly expanded from architect and client to friend and friend. Dr. Spivey had a great dream but no money. However, he was a talented fund raiser. He imbued people with his own enthusiasm for whatever he was undertaking in behalf of his college.

Mr. Wright created a master plan for the campus, designed as separate buildings connected together throughout a citrus grove by means of concrete, shaded esplanades. The Anne Pfeiffer Chapel was built first, followed by a library, a group of seminar buildings, and an administration building. All of these were based on the master plan that Mr. Wright laid out in 1938. During the subsequent twenty years, other additions were made according to the plan. A science building was constructed as well as a minor chapel and an industrial arts complex. The raising of the necessary funds for the college building program was a constant task for Dr. Spivey, and it meant that many times his architect had to wait patiently for his fees. But Mr. Wright had great faith in Dr. Spivey, just as the client did in his architect. They worked marvelously together, and, though there were several fine buildings that were not built, the campus remains today a remarkable example of an architecture indigenous to its environment. The net effect evokes an American atmosphere with style and form in perfect keeping with the twentieth century.

The Whitney Memorial, containing art galleries, studios, exhibition spaces, and residence for artists and faculty, terminates at the lake's edge with the Children's Building. It is the lovely and poetic Children's Building (plate 29) that is shown here simply because it is one of the most romantic and delicately imagined works by Mr. Wright. The building throughout is a fantasy for a child's enjoyment. Through the architectural setting, the child can begin to feel the forms and shapes of what constitutes organic architecture on a level that he or she can comprehend. It is actually the design of an earlier building conceived for Aline Barnsdall of Los Angeles (plates 9a, 9b). She had commissioned Mr. Wright for a small playhouse-theatre, and he created a work that he called "The Little Dipper." The project consists of a long wing extended out from a square form, similar in shape to the famous constellation. Miss Barnsdall eventually gave her Olive Hill property to the city of Los Angeles. At that time, the Little Dipper was under construction and the city, quite frankly, did not want it. Miss Barnsdall was outraged and demolished the basement terraces and retaining walls of the playhouse, converting the slab area into a park-terrace as a memorial to her father.

Now, twenty-one years later, Mr. Wright hoped to once again see the charming Little Dipper rise, as a Florida Southern building commissioned by Mr. and Mrs. Cornelius Vanderbilt Whitney as a memorial to Mrs. Payne Whitney. But the funds were never given by the Whitneys to the college. Perhaps like that of so many other donors, their taste in college architecture ran to the classical revivals and the Gothic and Romanesque styles that people in those days felt dignified higher education.

Gerald Loeb, of Wall Street's E. F. Hutton Company, had a cherubic face, round head balding at the top, and white-gray hair around his ears. Rather short and stocky, he wore black horn-rimmed glasses and looked not unlike Buckminster Fuller. He was a man of boundless enthusiasm and was a genius where the stock market was concerned. Loeb had married late in life a lovely redhead named Rose Benjamin, whose previous husband, Dr. Maurice Benjamin, had financed and built much of the Shanghai coast in China. Following her husband's death she emigrated from China and Australia to the United States where she met and married Mr. Loeb.

By the time of their marriage, Loeb was already a client of Mr. Wright's, commissioning a home to be built on a long hill ridge in Connecticut. The Loeb house (plate 30) appears, from the exterior, somewhat vast and imposing. But the scale is such that a man can reach up and touch the eaves everywhere, and the lighting is mostly from skylights in the roof. Under favorable conditions, the hill ridge affords an unbroken view down across fields, over dense forests, and to Long Island Sound almost forty miles away. The house is specifically designed to protect the inhabitants from the prevalent strong winds that sweep up, over, and across the hill crown.

Rose Loeb was against the house from the very beginning. They had spent a fortune remodeling a barn in the valley of his Connecticut estate, furnished it to resemble a Japanese home with shoji screens, tatami mats, and exquisite oriental works of art from Rose's stay in China. Loeb had also made the formidable mistake of taking the preliminaries of his home to a local Connecticut contractor for an estimate. Mr. Wright scolded him severely for taking the advice of a contractor who was not familiar with the construction techniques of a Frank Lloyd Wright design. But Loeb was convinced forever after that the house was going to cost him above and beyond the estimate that Mr. Wright had given him. Rose once said in defense of not building the project, "If I already have a fine mink coat, why should I go out and buy a sable"?

Mr. Loeb had the unfortunate knack of opening his mouth wide and placing his foot squarely within it. He managed to irritate Mr. Wright on more than one occasion. He once photographed, or had photographed, some eight hundred of Mr. Wright's original drawings without permission, with the intention of placing the negatives in a university. Loeb was forced to send the eight hundred negatives and all the prints to Taliesin.

Loeb delayed and postponed the decisions about his proposed home for a period of five or six years. And even though he authorized Mr. Wright to proceed with a full set of structural drawings, he never paid his fee in full. "Dear GM," Mr. Wright then wrote, "For a man who has so much, you have so little. . . . You only go to prove that more is less." However, a few weeks after that letter, Mr. and Mrs. Loeb wrote that they were coming west to Arizona, and Mr. Wright invited them to stay with him, saying, "Olgivanna and I look greatly forward to seeing you and your Rose, and hope you will plan to stay with us on the guest deck at Taliesin. . . . Affection, Frank."

Rose was a delightful and warmhearted person, and socially the Wrights and the Loebs got along quite well. But with Loeb, as with many Frank Lloyd Wright clients, the going could get rough, especially where the integrity of the building, of the work of architecture, was concerned. Mr. Wright protected his work fiercely, but at the same time had an inborn affection and respect for his friends. And when clients became friends, he was devoted to them, as they were to him.

"SUNLIGHT," DESERT SPA FOR ELIZABETH ARDEN
PHOENIX, ARIZONA, 1945

No explanation of this particular project (plate 31), designed for the famous cosmetic manufacturer and racing horse owner Elizabeth Arden, could better reveal the situation of the commission and its resultant refusal than when Frank Lloyd Wright wrote:

Elizabeth Arden made an excursion to Taliesin West with the high purpose of doing something for her clientele in the Arizona desert as inspiring in point of appropriate relationship to environment as is her practice with female reconstitution. Soon, all mixed up where that affair was concerned, we lost sight of her. But what we did for her, on the spur of that moment, is included here for your entertainment. The arrangement is sufficiently obvious, the roof in this instance becoming earth-on-terrace and developing as an over-all garden, the owner in residence bringing up the rear. It would seem that the fundamental error in this essay lay in the emphasis placed on sunlight when twilight or moonlight was preferable. Project abandoned.

ADELMAN LAUNDRY, MILWAUKEE, WISCONSIN, 1945

Benjamin Adelman owned and operated a laundry and dry-cleaning business in Milwaukee that eventually expanded to several branch offices. In 1945, he asked Frank Lloyd Wright to design the main plant for him. He also asked Mr. Wright to design a home for himself in the suburbs north of Milwaukee on a lake-front site overlooking Lake Michigan. At the same time, his son Albert Adelman also requested a house design. Over the next six years, in addition to the laundry, Mr. Wright designed three homes for Benjamin Adelman, two for his son Albert, and one for Ben Feenberg, one of the officials in the Adelman Laundry. Of all these projects, one house was built for Albert at Fox Point, a suburb of Milwaukee, and one for his father in Phoenix, near the Arizona Biltmore Hotel.

Mr. Adelman always called his wife Mama, and she referred to him as Papa Adelman. In the course of their meetings with Mr. Wright, these salutations continued right on into the architect-client relations, and soon Mr. Wright found himself referring to them as clients Mother and Father Adelman. Son Albert was always referred to as Ollie. Adelman senior had great admiration and affection for Mr. Wright. Each winter, Mr. and Mrs. Adelman came to Phoenix and stayed at the Arizona Biltmore Hotel. They were invited frequently to Taliesin West, which in the mid 1940s was quite literally a camp: rock walls, redwood trusses, canvas stretched in frames overhead.

We generated our own electric current, light fixtures hung on lamp cords from the trusses above, heating was provided by butane gas heaters, and only four oil stoves heated the great drafting room. Mr. and Mrs. Wright used portable kerosene heaters in their quarters; the rest of us lived mainly in tents along the northwest boundary of the property, except for an apprentice court for the senior members of Taliesin. It was primitive in many ways but always exciting. Strong winter rain storms caused much leakage through the canvas overhead; winds cut through the openings between canvas flaps and stone walls. And through it all was a magnificent sense of grandeur and luxury. Weekend evenings were formal occasions when we gathered in Mr. and Mrs. Wright's living room, called the Garden Room, ate dinner in tuxedoes, performed our own music with our own chorus and chamber ensemble, which Mr. Wright lovingly and humorously referred to as the "farmer-labor quartet." Then throughout the week we continued work on the construction of Taliesin West as well as the architectural work at hand.

Naturally, the Adelmans were invited to these affairs, but it meant a drive of some fifteen miles across the desert on a road that was not much more than a rough gulley in the landscape. Washes filled with water during the rainy season, and the rocks and potholes in dry weather made the voyage seem like a ride on a bronco in a rodeo. It was a little too rough for Mother

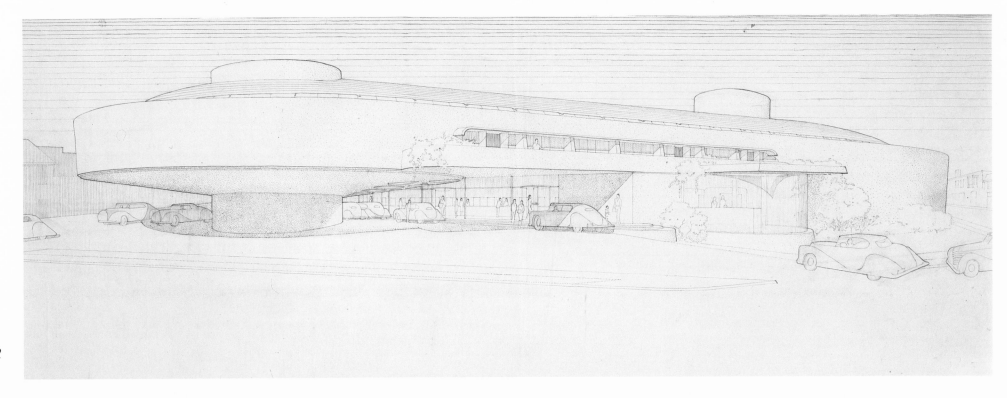

Adelman, and they invariably converted the invitation to come out to Taliesin West into one wherein the Wrights would come down for dinner to the elegant Gold Room of the Arizona Biltmore Hotel.

On one such evening at the Biltmore, during dinner Father Adelman turned to Mr. Wright and asked: "Mr. Wright, there is so much mystery about who designed this hotel, you or Albert Chase McArthur. Can't you clear it up once and for all?" Mr. Wright turned his head in a gesture of surveying the room in which they were dining, and replied: "Look around you, Father Adelman, the building speaks for itself." And with a smile he closed the subject.

The laundry (plate 32) was a fully worked-out project for which a complete set of working drawings was made. Even in those days, Mr. Wright was concerned about security features. The Adelmans, father and son, wondered at his concern, and Mr. Wright explained that since their service also included cold storage for furs, security was a must. The main dry-cleaning and laundry area is a large workroom with a plenum ceiling-roof—a large, tank-like structure that takes away the vast amount of steam and moisture that is prevalent in a laundry and dry-cleaning establishment. A mezzanine gallery contains a special dining area for staff and workers. Drive-in service was thoroughly provided for, as well as loading and unloading docks for the laundry's service trucks. All the walls are sleek, clean, smooth surfaces of reinforced concrete.

Unfortunately, at the time that the laundry was about to be built, the Adelmans, father and son (but mostly the son), decided to change their operation from one large new plant to a remodeling of their existing plant and the building of other small branch outlets around Milwaukee. That change of plans eliminated the need for Mr. Wright's design.

DAPHNE FUNERAL CHAPELS, SAN FRANCISCO, CALIFORNIA, 1945

Nicholas Daphne, a San Francisco mortician, turned the undertaking business into a thriving profession. Evelyn Waugh's *The Loved One* (1947) was written with him in mind, but a few years before he gained such recognition he employed Frank Lloyd Wright to design a group of funeral chapels and work areas on a San Francisco hill. Mr. Wright had never designed a funeral parlor before, and Mr. Daphne sent him many lists of requirements for work areas needed other than the chapels open to the general public.

When Mr. Wright first published the plans and perspective of the chapels, he wrote:

> Nicholas P. Daphne called me after midnight a year or so ago to say that because he had bought the finest lot in San Francisco he wanted the best architect in the world to build a mortuary on it. Nick asked me if I had ever built one. I said no, and I thought that was my very best qualification for doing one. So he gave me the job. Of course I had to "research" a good deal and that nearly got me down. I would come back home, now and then, wondering if I felt as well as I should. But Nick had a way of referring to the deceased always as the merchandise, and that would cheer me up.

The designs got as far as full presentation drawings, worked out in full detail. The chapels were planned as a cluster of five smaller chapels (plate 33), each seating up to one hundred people in separate gardens surrounded by a larger garden. Preparation of the deceased is relegated to a lower level, actually a basement area in the hill itself with underground access to the city street. Offices, casket display, and flower shops are in an adjacent building not connected to the chapels. Two of the chapels could be opened to each other so as to accommodate a funeral requiring seating for two hundred persons. Slumber rooms for the chief mourners are adjacent to the chapel, where the family could have privacy during the funeral service yet be able to see the casket in the chapel. The scale of the entire ensemble is human. The gardens are an ever-present feature, necessary to place emphasis, as Mr. Wright said, "not on Death, but on Life, with every possible convenience designed to make the place more helpful to the bereaved."

Daphne also asked Mr. Wright to design a home for the suburbs near San Francisco, but neither the chapels nor the home was ever built, even though working drawings were prepared.

34

It was rather late one evening at Taliesin when the telephone rang. Frank Lloyd Wright himself picked up the receiver, and, after Mrs. V. C. Morris explained that she was calling from San Francisco, she went on to say, "I know that this is really calling out of the blue, Mr. Wright, but my husband and I have just acquired some property near Golden Gate Bridge on the bay and would dearly love to have you design a house for us." When Mr. Wright inquired about the size of the property there was a bit of a delay in the response and then, "It seems to be about 90 feet on the roadside edge of the land." "I am sorry, Mrs. Morris, but it is a long-standing rule of mine not to build on city lots. You would find such a piece of land too confining for what I would design. I would suggest you look for more acreage elsewhere. But thank you anyway for calling." Mr. Wright hung up and prepared to retire for the evening.

The phone rang again and it was Mrs. Morris's voice again, sounding out of breath and extremely anxious. "I am afraid I misrepresented our property to you, Mr. Wright. It does measure 90 feet on the road edge, but the land is fan shaped and extends out of the sea front with a long sweep of water's edge beneath the cliff. It is a most dramatic site. You would love it and are the only person who could do it justice." "That would change the situation considerably, Mrs. Morris. Send me a list of your requirements along with a topographical survey of the site and we'll see what we can do." "What we can do" turned into one of the most poetic and inspiring of all

the residential designs created by Frank Lloyd Wright.

The Morrises owned and operated a gift shop in downtown San Francisco. Later on, they would commission Mr. Wright to design for them the now-famous V. C. Morris Shop on chic Maiden Lane. In fact, it was the designing and building of the gift shop that kept postponing the construction of their cliff-top home near Golden Gate Bridge. Often Mr. Wright referred to this action of building one design, the lesser, before going on to build the other, the greater, as "the steamboat that blew its whistle, and had to head back for shore for more wood to build up more steam!"

On the road edge, the home (plate 34) appears to be a low garden wall. The top of the building is a garden terrace covering an open loggia passage between the street side, with its garage and entry drive, and the house itself, which clings to the cliff edge and plunges down to the water below in concentric circles of reinforced concrete. Because of its location as a cliff-side home, the plan is basically stacked: one circular level above a square one, containing four levels in all, terminating with the roof garden on top. The stack of floors is interconnected by means of ramps descending along an open well, the uppermost level being a conservatory for plants and vines. This open well ramp is thus turned into a hanging garden four floors deep. Broad overhangs protect generous sheets of fixed and swinging sash that look out over San Francisco Bay. Reinforced concrete and steel are combined in such a way as to make this

building both fireproof and earthquake-proof. The upper garden level, with its large, extended terrace, acts as insulation for the house from the sun and rain. Smaller, more intimate balconies protrude from the various levels off the living room, study, dining room, and bedrooms below.

The house was designed in 1945, the complete set of working drawings signed in April 1946. But construction was delayed even further as the work went on for the Morris Gift Shop. This occupied the Morrises for the next few years, and it seemed as though the house was put aside for good.

To reduce construction costs, Mr. Wright made another proposal to the Morrises: place the house farther down the slope, half way between the upper cliff edge and the water below and nestled into the cliff's slope. He made another set of presentation drawings, with an elevator tower on the upper part of the property to gain access to the house half way down the cliff, this time more horizontal in character.

Sea Cliff was again rejected by the Morrises, and ten years later, in 1954, they asked Mr. Wright to design for them a guest house on that same site.

SARABHAI CALICO MILLS STORE, AMEHABAD, INDIA, 1945

After the end of the Second World War, many new students from overseas came to study with Frank Lloyd Wright. From India came several, among them a young woman named Gira Sarabhai. Her family owned and operated cotton mills in India and soon after her arrival at Taliesin, followed by the arrival of her brother as well, her father Gautam Sarabhai became interested in having Mr. Wright design a department store for his calico mills in Amehabad, India.

The climate of India being predominantly hot and humid, the design that Mr. Wright worked out (plate 35a) takes into consideration first of all the circulation of air within the building. Several stories tall, the central portion of the store is open to form a large and spacious well, lit from above. A smaller open well provides for further air circulation. The floors themselves not only look over and into these wells but at the edges of the exterior wall are kept free from the wall itself. This permits a passage of air up the well and around the floor edges, designed as one gentle flow in contrast to the intermittent blasts of air conditioning.

Air conditioning in 1945 was rare in the West, let alone in India. Moreover, Mr. Wright felt that air conditioning is usually too strong, too cold, and in dangerous contrast to the air of the out-of-doors. He considered it unhealthy for human beings to come suddenly from a very high temperature into a very cold one. In the proposed Amehabad store, the air is supplied from the shafts running along the elevator shaft. It is then directed out along the periphery of the wall on each floor level and allowed to circulate by means of gravity throughout the open wells and open slab edges.

The exterior walls, made of concrete block with glass inserts, become virtually protective curtains forming a shield for the interior spaces. Like hanging curtains, these walls do not support the floor slabs, which are independent of them.

The store window on the street below is treated in a manner that Mr. Wright had been trying to get built for many years, ever since 1923 when he designed a merchandising building for Los Angeles (plate 35b). The problem with the average shop window is that with a necessary overhang to protect pedestrians from sun and rain, the window becomes, in the bright light, very dark, almost black, acting thus as a mirror. It requires strong artificial lighting to counteract this natural condition. In the merchandising building that he designed in 1923, intended for the sun-drenched climate of southern California, he let the window extend up behind the sunscreen-overhang to another level. It could then turn over in bays of mitred glass to become a skylight, adjustable for density and brightness by louvers and screens. As a result, the window's contents are generously lighted by natural daylight, and the window shoppers outside are amply protected. The light from above would automatically cancel the otherwise disturbing mirror effect.

In the Sarabhai Calico Mills Store, the long, colorful bolts of brightly dyed cloth are shown in a tall display area, seen in the perspective, with large hanging sweeps of color fabric. The sixth floor is a garden-terrace restaurant. Two floors above that level are reserved for offices and a penthouse.

The work approached working drawing stage and plans were sent to India for some preliminary estimates. The innovative system of air conditioning, combined with the use of reinforced concrete cantilevered slabs and the concrete curtain wall, were so far in advance of what the Indian engineers and builders could comprehend that the project was deemed incomprehensible and thus abandoned.

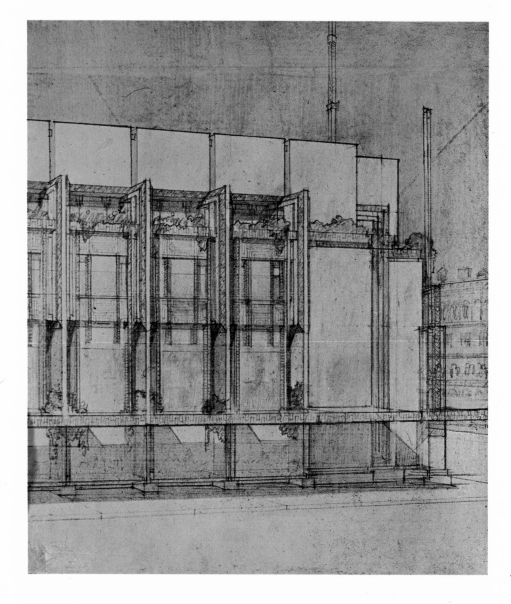

35b

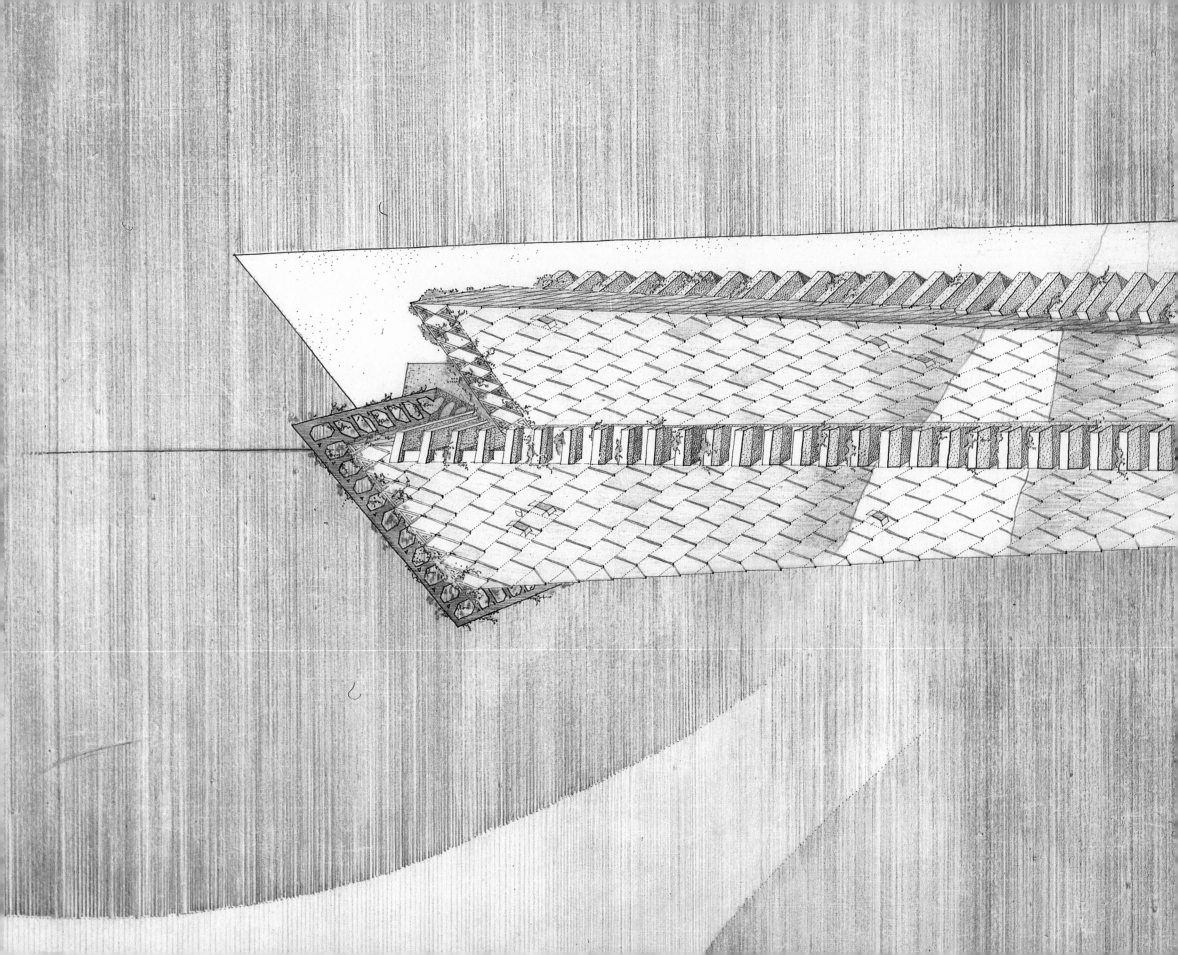

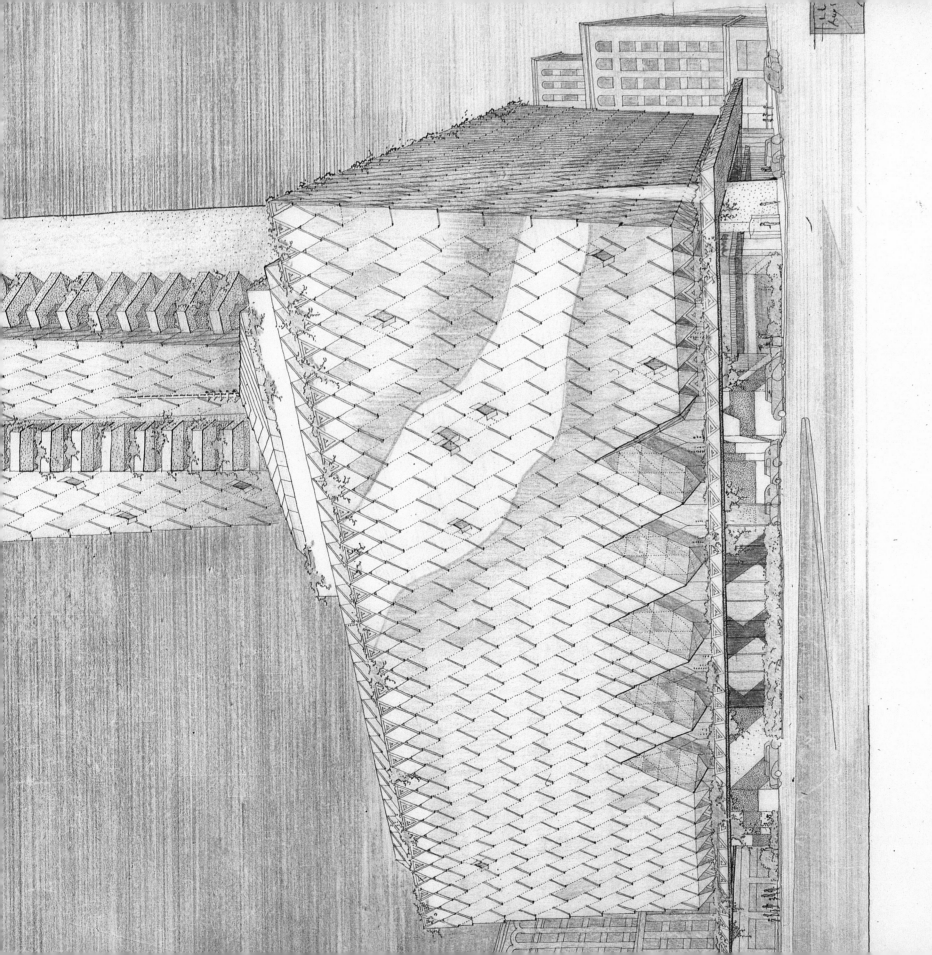

36a

36b

ROGERS LACY HOTEL, DALLAS, TEXAS, 1946

In several major cities throughout the world, we now see hotels employing the idea of a central atrium-court, sometimes open to the sky above or closed, depending upon the location and its climate. Many older hotels, such as the Brown Palace in Denver, Colorado, set the rooms around an open court rising in tiers of balconies. But the use of the atrium-court in modern structures came out of the design that Mr. Wright made for this particular hotel (plate 36c).

The Rogers Lacy Hotel (plate 36a) was designed to occupy a full city block in downtown Dallas. Its exterior wall surface is composed of glass triangular panels, two layers in thickness, with an air-space in between filled with glass wool insulation. In some instances, these panels could open, but in general it was planned for them to remain closed, the light coming through being softly translucent. Downtown Dallas, with its predominantly muggy and sultry climate, is not conducive to a view as such, and so the impulse to seek an outdoor view is minimized. On the atrium-court side of the building, however, the rooms open onto sun-balconies overlooking the courtyard, balconies generously planted with shrubs and flowers.

The first nine floors of the hotel extend to the full size of the city block. An additional fifty-five stories rise out of this mass at one corner, designed to contain condominiums, apartments, and larger suites. Ground level is devoted to public rooms, a large space designed mostly as one entire room with movable partitions. An automobile entrance comes in under the protection of the floors above (plate 36b), with ramps down to underground parking facilities. Lobbies, coffee shops, restaurants, bars, and cafes are placed on this ground level, grouped around the central atrium with its water gardens and luxurious planting (plate 36c). Private banquet halls, convention rooms, concessions such as beauty parlors, barber shops, floral shops, and so forth are placed on the various nine floors above, along with the guest rooms. The guest rooms are arranged in

John Rosenfield was the art and architecture critic for the *Dallas Morning News* and a great champion of Frank Lloyd Wright. He had met the architect when Mr. Wright came to Dallas in the 1930s to work on a house for Stanley Marcus, son of the founder of Neiman-Marcus. The two men liked one another instantly, and Rosenfield was invited to come to Taliesin as Mr. Wright's house guest.

Following the termination of the war in 1945, a friend of John Rosenfield's, attorney Gordon Rupes, talked to him about the building boom going on in Dallas as a result of the vast oil millions being accumulated. One such person was his client, Rogers Lacy. A thin, smallish man, a most unlikely looking millionaire, he had made his fortune in oil rather late in life. He had made, he reported, "a bundle of money in oil, but one day recently when I actually sat down and took a tally of all I had made I discovered I was rich beyond my wildest imagination!" Rosenfield suggested to Rupes that Lacy would do well to build for his city a fine monument designed by the world's greatest architect. Acting on that advice, Lacy came to Mr. Wright and asked him to design a large hotel for downtown Dallas.

groups of four, accessed from the sun balconies, without interior corridors. In this way the usual space occupied by lengthy corridors has been abolished.

Where the ninth floor meets the tower, a cabaret is designed for dining and dancing, the roof of the cabaret rising in crystalline forms to be anchored in the tower alongside.

The first basement, directly beneath the ground level, is devoted in its entirety to the kitchens, food storage and preparation, and service elevators. These elevators service the entire building, including the tower. Each floor area above has smaller kitchens serviced by these elevators, to keep food warm and to service each floor independently.

The tower, a tall shaft of concrete cantilevers, is based on the St. Mark's project of 1929, and a similar application of it was built in Bartlesville, Oklahoma, in 1953 for the H. C. Price Company. Some of the apartments occupy one floor, others are duplex. The shaft rising alongside the glass-surfaced tower contains the utilities and elevator banks, as well as acting as the structurally stabilizing element for the tower. The glass areas here, as well as in the main hotel block below, are double-thickness glass or plexiglass. With insulation in between the two layers, the light is translucent. Certain panels open for the view as wished and for fresh air as desired.

Over forty preliminary presentation drawings were made for this carefully worked out hotel, but before the decision was made to go into the working drawing stage for the building, the client died and the project was abandoned. It remains to this day one of the truly great, creative, and innovative designs by Mr. Wright.

DR. ALFRED BERGMAN HOUSE, ST. PETERSBURG, FLORIDA, 1947

Every client who built a Frank Lloyd Wright house has, invariably, the deep conviction that the house that Mr. Wright designed and built for him or her was his best, his masterpiece. His aim was to make every one of his homes a building that would not only give shelter to the client but would make him or her feel instantly at home and at ease within it. His sense of human scale was his most prevalent guideline when designing for human habitation, and therefore he shunned unnecessary heights and widths. He scaled his homes to fit the human beings who were to live in them.

He placed his homes in the landscape, not on it. Where there was a special feature of the site, a cliff, a forest, a spectacular overlook, a brook, whatever circumstance of nature, that became the key to his way of thinking through his design and eventually it became the feature of the building itself. If a house is placed on top of the hill, then of course it follows that there is no hill left; it has been killed off. When he designed Fallingwater as a series of ledges and cantilevers projecting out over the water cascades, his client Edgar J. Kaufmann at first exclaimed: "I thought you would have me look at

my waterfall." Mr. Wright explained, "No, E. J., not just to look at it, I want you to live with it."

Alfred Bergman's house is for an ocean-side resort in St. Petersburg, Florida. The surrounding area being totally flat and built up by other housing, a view out and above is provided for the main living area with a screened and raised deck, seen on the perspective (plate 37) as the second story of the building. Bedrooms and guest rooms, along with the usual living, kitchen, and dining areas, are on the ground floor, facing an enclosed walled garden. In this manner the residents have the option of a fine and dramatic view from the pavilion above or a quiet and secluded atmosphere on the water's edge with its private garden.

This house developed out of a scheme Mr. Wright designed first for Florida Southern College president Ludd M. Spivey, to be built in Venice-like Fort Lauderdale. The Bergman house never went beyond preliminary presentation drawings, but from the working drawings of the Spivey house we can get a clear idea of how Mr. Wright wished to see the building constructed. Particularly interesting are the specially cast perforated concrete blocks and the delicate, metal, trellislike supports that hold the roof over the second-story pavilion.

E. L. MARTING HOUSE, NORTHAMPTON, OHIO, 1947

The solar hemicycle designed and built for Herbert Jacobs near Madison, Wisconsin, was a revolution in what is today called passive solar planning. Rather than using the complex and often ugly apparatus required to take heat from the sun, store it, and use it within the house, solar hemicycle planning for this house for E. L. Marting (plate 38) as well as for the Jacobs house makes use of the site and the sun taken together.

Earth bermed up on the north, the cold side of the house, keeps the interior warm in winter and cool in summer. The half-circle, called hemicycle, area of tall glass windows on the south welcomes the sun's rays during winter but is protected by an overhanging roof in the summertime. A carefully planned embankment of earth on a low mound in front of the hemicycle, in plan actually completing the circle, prevents strong winds from hitting the large glass areas during winter storms. The slight rise of banking deflects the winds up and over the roof's edge, thus avoiding direct, head-on contact with the windows.

The Marting house is larger and more elegantly developed than the Jacobs house, since the Jacobs house was not only the prototype but designed to be built on a most stringent budget. Although Marting never built this design, Mr. Wright continued to use the solar hemicycle in several other house projects, chiefly in the Midwest where winters are severe and where the concept of the berm and half-circle make for more comfortable habitation.

AYN RAND STUDIO-RESIDENCE, 1947

In 1937, novelist Ayn Rand wrote to Frank Lloyd Wright about her work on a new novel concerning the career of an architect. She made it clear that although she was not writing specifically about Mr. Wright, she was writing about a man who followed his own convictions throughout his life. "A man," she said, "who has an ideal and goes through hell for it. . . . His story is the story of human integrity. That is what I am writing. That is what you have lived. And to my knowledge you are the only one among the men of this century who has lived it." She requested an interview with Mr. Wright, hoping to come to Taliesin at Spring Green, Wisconsin. At that moment, however, Mr. Wright was in Arizona searching for a site for the building of Taliesin West.

The following year, Miss Rand once again introduced herself in a letter in which she recalled their meeting at a dinner party in New York. And once again she requested the chance to come and visit Mr. Wright. She sent him a copy of her novel *We the Living* as well as the first several chapters of the new work about the architect. "These, I think," she wrote, "will be the best references that I can offer you. If you will glance through them you will be able to decide whether I am a writer good enough to deserve any further consideration from you. . . . If you do not approve at all—please let me know that, because then I'll stop torturing myself with attempts to reach you and I will have to proceed on the novel without the thing I would like to have—your blessing on my undertaking."

Mr. Wright read through the outline she sent and replied to Miss Rand: "Dear Ayn Rand: No man named Roarke with flaming red hair could be a genius that could lick the contracting confraternity. Both obstruct themselves disagreeably and he is not very convincing. Will try to find time to see you in New York and say why if you want me to do so." When she telegraphed for a definite appointment, Mr. Wright had again gone to Arizona, and the two did not meet for many years. Her book *The Fountainhead* was published in 1943 and immediately became popular throughout the nation. At that time they finally met in Hollywood, where Miss Rand was making arrangements for the film version of her book. Mr. Wright went frequently to California to work for various clients. His son Lloyd was a practicing architect

in Beverly Hills and his granddaughter, Anne Baxter, lived in Hollywood and introduced him to many of the stars, directors, and producers that were her friends.

During one meeting with Miss Rand, Mr. Wright told her: "If you and I were living in the Renaissance, they would burn us as heretics!" "Not me," she retorted, "I don't burn!"

She wrote to him again in May 1944 concerning the filming of her book, and in the same letter she said, "Now, would you be willing to design a house for me? You said you had to be interested in a person before you accepted him or her as a client."

After that, a year passed without further correspondence from Miss Rand. Then in the summer of 1945 she wrote to thank Mr. Wright for an autographed copy of one of his books and reminded him that she still wanted a Frank Lloyd Wright house of her own. She was headed for New York and intended to purchase land. Mr. Wright invited her to stop at Taliesin on her way from California to the East Coast. She and her husband spent several days in Wisconsin. Yet, one year later, she wrote from California: "I will not be able to come east this year to look for the land—and I don't want my choice of the land to be rash, since that will be my permanent home. So are you still willing to grant me the exception of a house designed ahead of the site?" A week or so later, Mr. Wright wrote: "Dear Ayn Rand: We are sending on to you a scheme for a compact dwelling for a writer who loves the idea of organic architecture and won't take less for a home [plate 39]. It can be built with a few minor changes in Connecticut, Texas, Arizona or Florida."

"The house you designed for me is magnificent," Miss Rand replied after the drawings reached her. She specified some small changes but was delighted with the "particular kind of sculpture in space which I love and which nobody but you has ever been able to achieve."

She suggested several other "minor" changes and asked to visit Mr. Wright at Taliesin West during the winter of 1947. The scheme seemed too large for her, she thought at that time, but her "minor changes" consisted of enlarging certain rooms within the building. Finally, she made up her mind about the location of her homesite, namely, Manhattan. In the center of New York City she would be surrounded by her literary friends, the connections and colleagues of her career. She abandoned once and for all the idea of a home in the country.

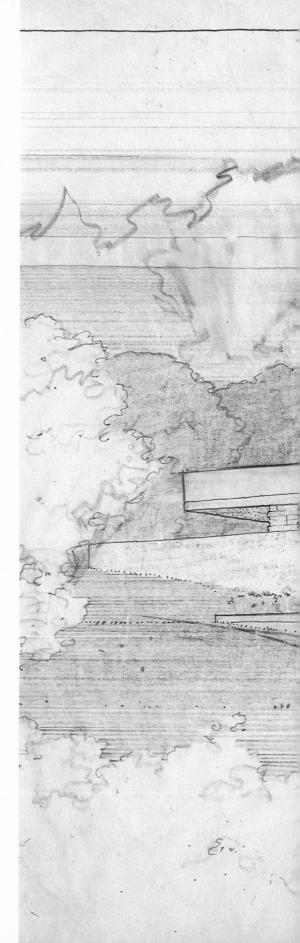

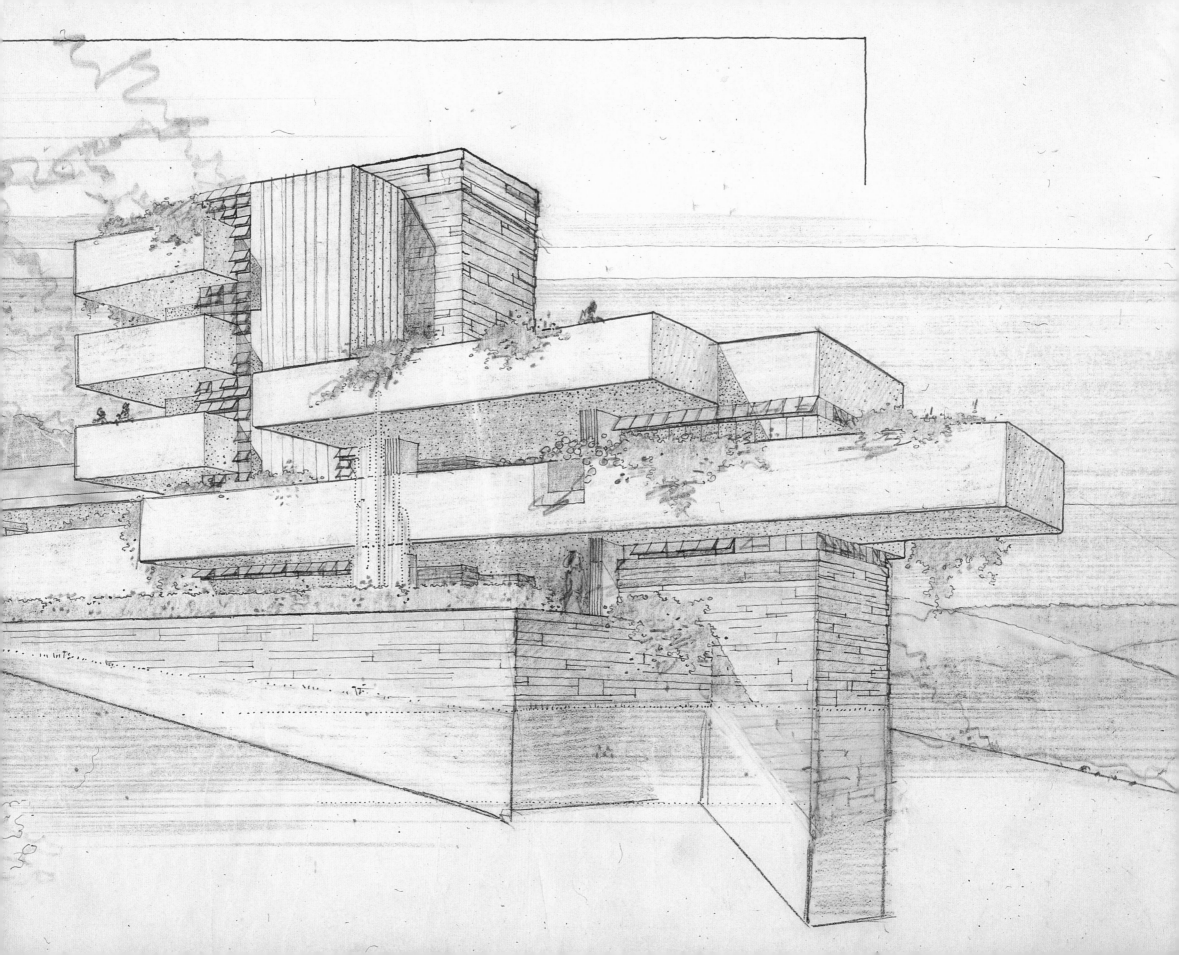

40

HUNTINGTON HARTFORD SPORTS CLUB
HOLLYWOOD, CALIFORNIA, 1947

On the sunset terrace at Taliesin West is a memorial that Mr. Wright designed and built for Mrs. Wright's daughter Svetlana, who was killed in an automobile accident in September 1946. The memorial consists of three plowshares made of turquoise-painted steel placed at equal points from one another on the lines of an equilateral triangle. They are supported a few feet off the terrace floor by means of a stone and concrete pylon. The pylon rises through discs in the center to hold a large Arizona quartz crystal over which a small fountain emerges and feeds water into the discs. Sometimes fresh flowers and foliage are placed on the discs for special occasions, such as the traditional Taliesin Easter breakfast, which is held on this terrace.

Some time after the memorial was built, Mr. Wright remarked that the form of those three discs projecting out of the central masonry core would be a good shape for a work of architecture. In 1947, he did indeed design a structure based on that form: the Sports Club for Huntington Hartford (plate 40), to be built in a canyon in Hollywood Hills, California. The Sports Club, or Play Resort as it is sometimes called, was to be part of a larger development that would include a hotel, riding stables, private residences, and canyon trails.

The Play Resort is in reality a private club with provision for tournament tennis and swimming. The Sports Club proper rides along the ridge of one of the canyon's hills, its three discs cantilevered dramatically over the surrounding tree tops. On the entrance level, the central masonry mass that rises up to carry and support the discs contains an entry loggia, business office, and card rooms. Going down one level, one reaches the dressing rooms and locker rooms, with access to the large swimming pool where water jets provide a continuing cascade over the edge and into the canyon below. Another level down the central mass holds various game rooms, with access on this level to the main tennis court and bleachers.

On the main level, which holds the three large discs, is provision for dining and dancing, for a cinema-cabaret, and for a general lounge. Each of the three discs has an outer-edge balcony for viewing the canyon and is roofed with glass tubes to give a crystalline, soft overhead light by day. At night the effect is reversed, and the discs appear to glow.

The project was defeated mainly by the zoning restrictions in the Hollywood Hills. Most of the land in that area was owned by various film stars who simply did not want a resort area in their midst. Of course, zoning laws were not as stringent as they later became, and the project could have been pushed through had there been more pressure on the part of the client.

As we look at this project today, almost forty years have passed, and it still appears like something from another planet. At first glance it has a certain "outer-space" look about it, but it is, in reality, fully appropriate to time and place, then as well as now.

HUNTINGTON HARTFORD HOUSE
HOLLYWOOD, CALIFORNIA, 1947

Part way up the canyon wall, near the lower level of the Play Resort property and the Sports Club on the crest above, Huntington Hartford was to have his own home. This design was based on a house originally proposed to a client named Ralph Jester. It was to be the first circular house designed by Frank Lloyd Wright, a design doomed never to be built during Mr. Wright's lifetime—although it was offered to many clients. Here again (plate 41) it was proposed, almost ten years after its first conception. The living room is a complete sphere, the lower part extending down the canyon wall, the part above to be made with glass tubing for sparkling, but diffused, lighting.

Along with the Play Resort and the Sports Club, the residence was finally abandoned, owing to the client's lack of interest in or enthusiasm for the designs. The Jester house, however, was finally built in 1971 and is a landmark for visitors from all over the world. It is placed fittingly on property near Taliesin West and is owned by the Frank Lloyd Wright Foundation.

41

VALLEY NATIONAL BANK–DAYLIGHT BANK, TUCSON, ARIZONA, 1947

Walter Bimson, president of the Valley National Bank in Phoenix, Arizona, gave an address to the Fine Arts Club Dinner on April 1, 1954, during which he recounted his first meeting with Frank Lloyd Wright:

> I had been aware of Frank Lloyd Wright many years before I met him. He walked unannounced into my office one day some twenty years ago, wearing a dark blue cape, his curled-brim hat, his cane hung upon his arm, with a jaunty and slightly haughty air. I called him by name and introduced myself. He accepted my recognition without surprise. We had not talked ten minutes until he informed me that he knew all about bankers and didn't like them. I responded that I had read his autobiography, knew all about his troubles with bankers and their like, but doubted if the artist and the banker could ever quite agree.
>
> Frank Lloyd Wright has doubtless forgotten this incident, but if he remembered it he would understand why I value so highly one of his recent books which he gave me with the inscription, "To Walter Bimson—a humane banker—believe it or not—Frank Lloyd Wright."

In 1947, Bimson asked Mr. Wright to design two banks for him, one for Sunnyslope, a suburb north of Phoenix, which would also be part of a shopping center as one design, the other, a bank for his Tucson branch of which there might eventually be several modeled after the first one. Mr. Wright called the bank for Tucson "The Daylight Bank" (plate 42) because of its central lighting coming in from above through diffused plastic. The Daylight Bank was called, on the plans, "Flexible Pattern," meaning that it could be of varying size depending upon the special requirements of the area it was to serve. The plan is basically a circle with a hexagonal roof made of concrete, glass, plastic, and copper. The main floor counters are placed around the periphery of the circle. A mezzanine balcony holds special spaces for loan offices and other consultation requirements. Below, in the basement, are the main vault, restrooms, and a safety deposit vault. The only glass area is at the front entrance, the lighting coming mainly from above. On the main floor level, an open well looks down to the lower level, making the entire interior one clear space, divided as required.

The materials are roman brick, a soft beige color, white concrete with aggregate chips of Arizona quartz mixed into the surface coat, copper trim for the plexiglass skylight roof panels, marble and onyx for the countertops, bronze for the gates and grilles—in every way very elegant, spacious, and airy. But at the same time its outside appearance is solid and strong. "A bank should look like a strong box, give a person a sense of security and protection for his money and valuables," Mr. Wright remarked to Bimson, "but also be human and spacious within for the workers and the customers."

One feature of the design is a series of six windows along the curved rear wall of the building which would serve as drive-in teller windows. This element caused no end of consternation among the bank officials. They protested that the idea of driving up to a bank was preposterous. Banking, they said, would always be done inside the bank by pedestrians. Mr. Wright tried to convince them that future banking would include drive-in capability; he kept the drive-in windows. He also insisted on ramps everywhere, so that banking would be easier for the handicapped and the elderly.

Bimson was by nature a conservative person, and these revolutionary concepts quite frankly alarmed him. He was also worried about the cost involved in building an unconventional structure. Although the working drawings were complete, construction was delayed for two years while Bimson deliberated about the possibility of looking foolish in the public eye.

Although Mr. Wright tried to convince him of the soundness of the bank design, his efforts were to no avail. He continued to be his friend and did business with him at the Valley National Bank, but he never became his architect in anything more than name.

42

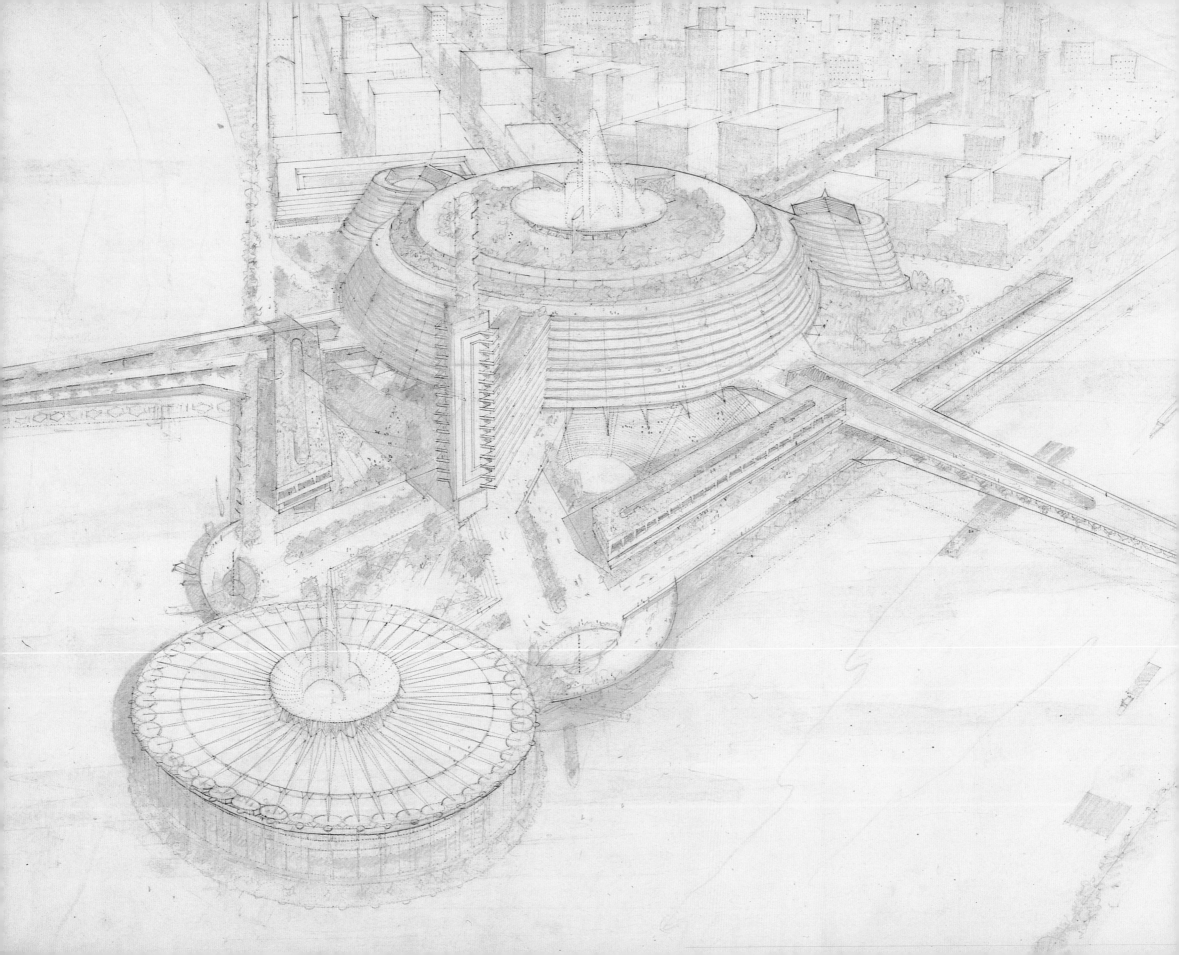

The idea for a civic center of mammoth proportions began with Edgar J. Kaufmann, Sr., the department store magnate for whom Frank Lloyd Wright built Fallingwater. Kaufmann was a cultivated man of great charm, who was affable, handsome, and liked by all. "My money has bought me many, many things in my life" he once told Mr. Wright, "but none of them have given me the deep pleasure that your house on Bear Run [Fallingwater] has given me."

In 1935, Kaufmann wanted the city of Pittsburgh to commission Mr. Wright to design and supervise a traffic control network for the Point Park, an area that had steadily deteriorated as a result of the encroachment of heavy industry. Most American cities, using their rivers to serve commerce, had destroyed both river and waterfront. Factories polluting the water and ships mooring up to ugly warehouses describe the usual fate of a city's water edge. Chicago, an exception, had made a beautiful feature of Lake Michigan by bordering the water with spacious parks and grassy areas. On the other hand, Pittsburgh had let its industrial buildings disfigure the natural point where its two rivers, the Allegheny and the Monongahela, meet. It had further marred its rivers by throwing hideous, steel-cage bridges across them. Too, it had allowed heavy industrial plants to spring up practically in the very heart of the city, dangerously close to the general commercial and cultural center of the city.

Air pollution had become so severe in this city of coal and steel production that when Mr. Wright visited Pittsburgh in the early thirties and gave a talk to the citizens, his solution for the city's problem was, quite simply and caustically, "The future of Pittsburgh? Abandon it!" But in a later meeting, arranged by Kaufmann, he explained that Pittsburgh must come to grips with the toxic smoke and fumes by zoning and restricting the building of heavy industrial plants or else the city would soon become a deathtrap. Pittsburgh did indeed do just that. The city fathers decided to make a park out of the point where the two rivers met and set up a commission called the Allegheny Conference to look into the possibilities of saving the area.

Even before he commissioned Mr. Wright to design Fallingwater, Kaufmann was anxious to have a feasible Frank Lloyd Wright civic plan for Pittsburgh. He had shown interest in urban problems and had financed the construction of the model for Broadacre City in 1934. Broadacre City was Mr. Wright's design for a city that was interspersed with the landscape, making the best features and beauty of the landscape part of the city itself. It was, in reality, no city at all in the usual sense of the word but a planned and studied aggregation of those buildings and dwellings necessary to human lives where they must congregate together for business and pleasure. The automobile had freed the American citizen from the obsolescence of the medieval city. No longer was it necessary to band together behind a high wall for protection from one's enemies. Quite the contrary, the cluttered, crowded, polluted city had become, and continues to be, the enemy to mankind, if human values are to be of any concern whatsoever.

The fluidity made possible by the automobile, with each person mobile and capable of almost infinite exploration along a horizontal plane, was the factor that made Broadacre City a flowing counterpart to its natural landscape. The same fluidity was the factor that would make the Pittsburgh civic center likewise accessible and flexible.

Mr. Wright prepared an extensive set of preliminary drawings for the Pittsburgh Point Park Civic Center in 1947 (plates 43a–43d) and made a further revision the following year (plates 44a, 44b). In both cases, the basic plan is a great circular ramped structure that is bordered by a triangular form created on one edge by the Monongahela River and on the other edge by the Allegheny River, while the third edge consists of city streets and pedestrian walks which offer access to the Center. Rising fifteen levels, the main circular structure that houses the various facilities of the civic center is a ramp bordered on the outer edge by planting and shrubs. This great ramp provides access to functions within the civic center, including parking. The peripheral planting is designed to soften the effect of the concrete, keep down the traffic noise, and absorb the fumes from cars.

The open ground level is an enormous traffic concourse, directing the flow of cars and trucks from the Pittsburgh city streets either to the upper and lower parking levels or out on either side to bridges that span the rivers. The outside edge of the Grand Ramp also contains two smaller circular structures, tangent in two places to the building for quick access to the civic and cultural facilities contained within the Grand Ramp structure itself. When the drawings were prepared and sent for presentation, Mr. Wright prepared a text explaining the project:

> The cantilever is employed by means of prestressed steel or cold drawn mesh cast in high pressure concrete with vertical and horizontal glass enclosures: a characteristic employment of steel in tension in appropriate architectural forms. This overall building scheme provides newly spacious means of entertainment for the citizen seated in his motor car, winter or summer. A pleasurable use of that modern implement is here

designed instead of allowing it to remain the troublesome burden it has now become to the City. The forms here employed are essentially economical and satisfying where the nature of glass and steel, our modern miracles, are concerned: for instance, the sweeping ramps and inverted or tension domes. More important, an overall harmony throughout the entire scheme of construction is presented to the Allegheny Conference. Provision for abundant greenery to absorb noise and temper walls and humanize occupation is everywhere insisted upon. Direct contact of the site with the Allegheny and Monongahela rivers makes the free use of abundant, filtered water an economical contributing factor in the general architectural scheme. As component supporting parts of the great overall structure, exhibition galleries, planetarium, forums, great halls for symphony or chamber music, grand opera, and conventions of every description are provided for. All easy of access with ample parking facilities immediately above or below each. A great arena for games utilizes the central roof area of the grand ramp. A large area of green park is by this means thrown up and against the sky in comparatively clean air and with a wide prospect.

The Center is further provided with a great auto ramp, 4½ miles in length, rising 175 above street level, accommodating 1,500 vehicles at once, safely spaced and going up with the same number safely coming down. Two cantilever double-deck tunnel bridges cross the river in a single span—concrete masses modified by decorative greenery.

Realizing constantly throughout his design that the ever present problem is the automobile, he provides parking on a scale never before imagined. On the street level, beneath the grand ramp: twenty-three acres; on the level above the street: an additional thirty-eight acres. Lower level, thirty-one acres; subway level, where traffic lanes connect with the bridge, thirty-one acres.

"The entire scheme is arranged," he concluded, "with adequate trees, shrubs, grass and gardening, all of which taken in connection with the broad expanse of flowing river surface render the whole architectural mass gentle and humane."

Brilliant as this scheme was, and clearly of great benefit to the city, the project was rejected. It was done so by the powerful, monied interests in Pittsburgh, mainly because of anti-Semitism. They did not want Kaufmann involved in any way with a civic project. They preferred to remain "restricted" and therefore closed to Jewish investments.

Thus, Pittsburgh lost this great megastructure, which would have been the first of its kind in the world—a structure of such beauty and grandeur that the world would certainly have streamed to Pittsburgh to see, to perform within it, to be part of it, to experience it. It could have been in the category of a permanent world's fair or world trade center. It remains now one of the most intricate, complex, and detailed of all Mr. Wright's larger conceptions.

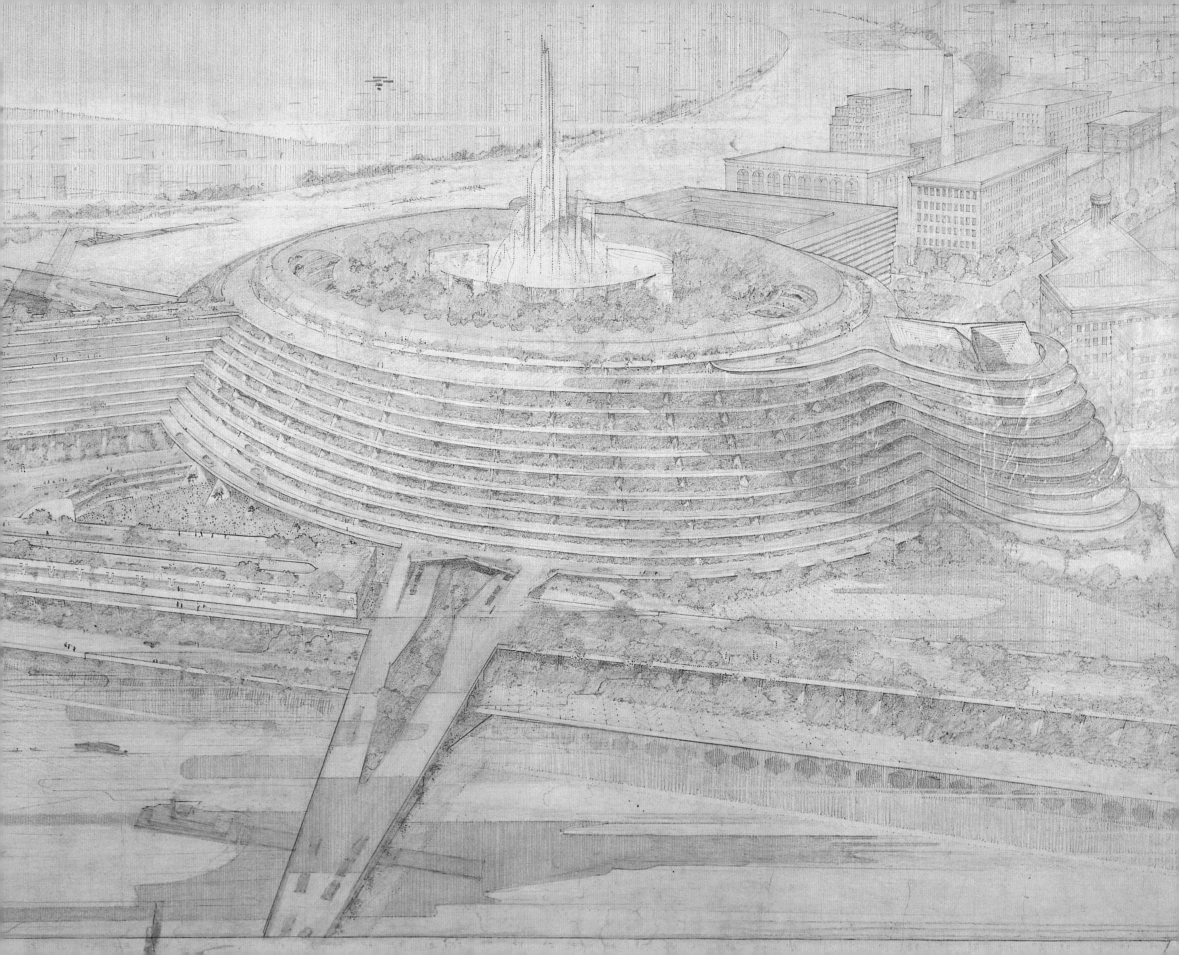

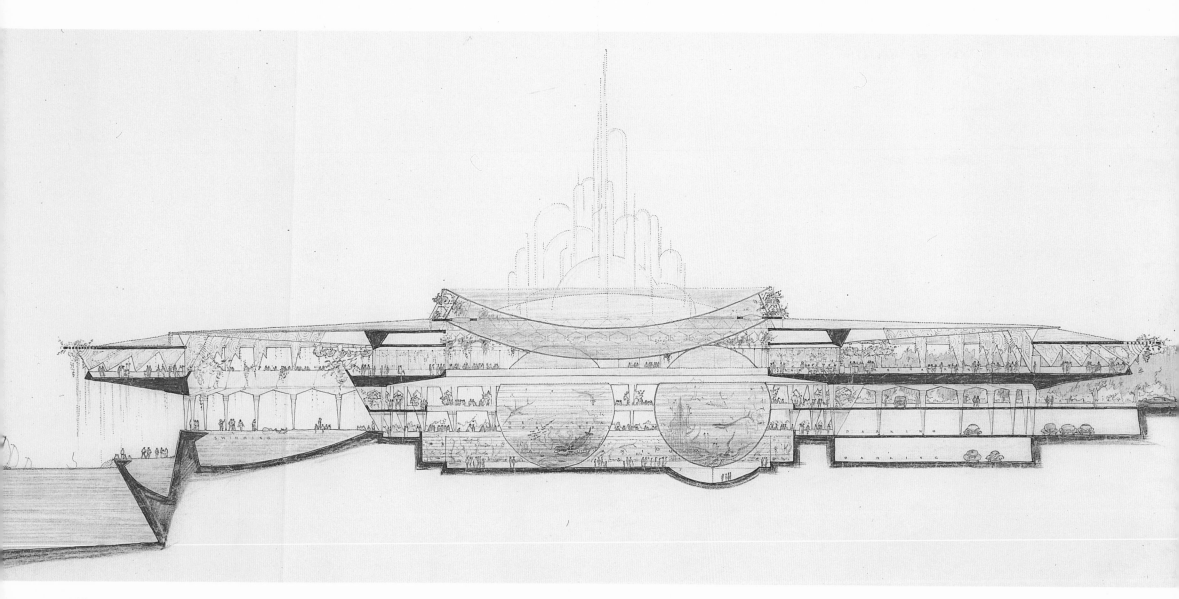

43c

43d

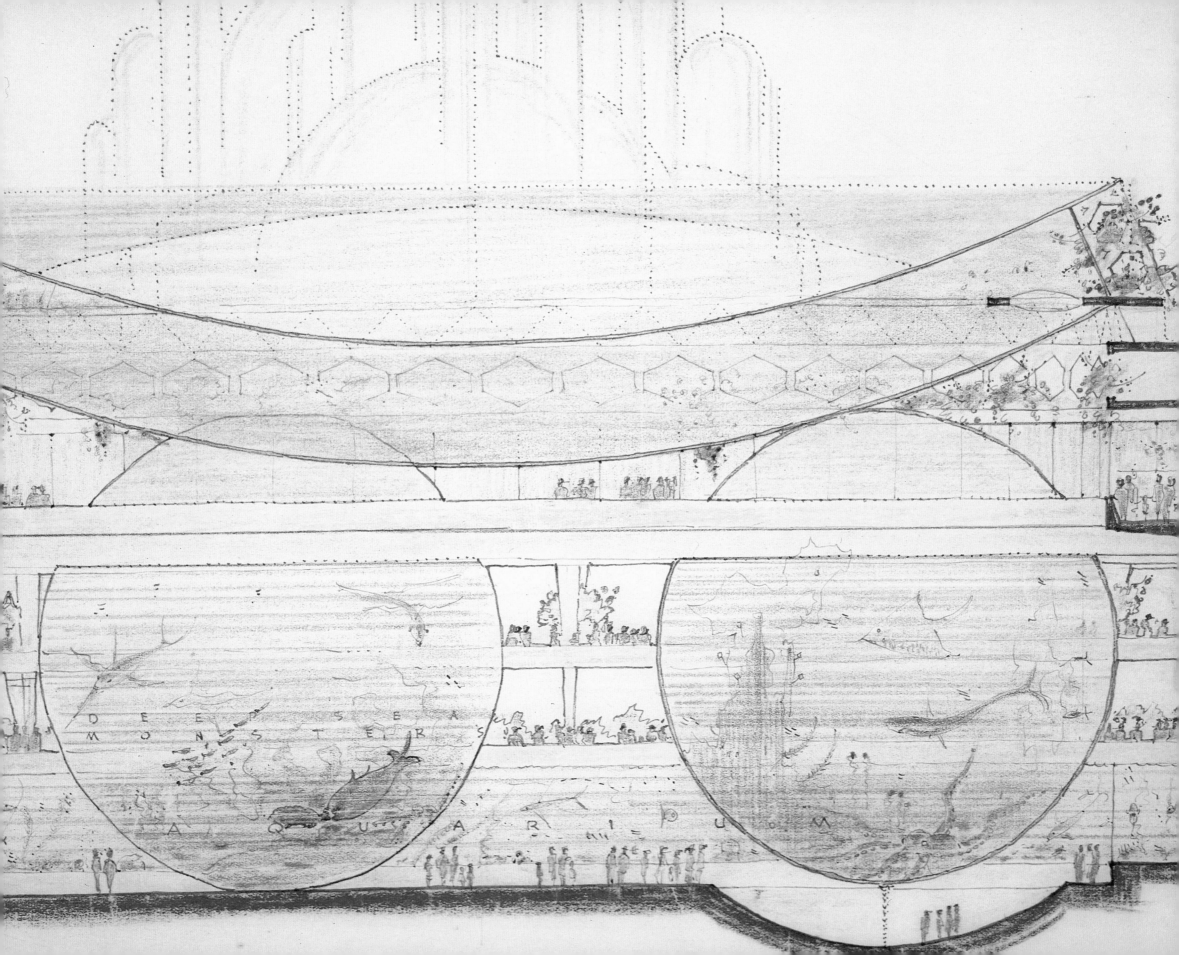

44b

TWIN CANTILEVERED BRIDGES AND CIVIC CENTER
PITTSBURGH, PENNSYLVANIA, 1947

The vast size and scope of Frank Lloyd Wright's first design for the Pittsburgh Civic Center proved to be too large for the city's requirements. Accordingly, Edgar J. Kaufmann, Sr., asked Mr. Wright to make a second proposal (plates 44a, 44b), with many of the center's functions and areas included from the specifications for scheme 1, but less complex. A principal concern in developing the Golden Triangle area, as it was called, was the traffic flow down to the point of the city and across the Allegheny and Monongahela rivers.

The second scheme features the two bridges required for the river crossings. In the design of any traffic pattern or roadbed, Mr. Wright maintained that so long as large trucks, commercial vehicles, and private vehicles were on the same roadway, the highway was obsolete from the very beginning. In the case of these bridges, three roadbeds are stacked, the lowest for trucks, the center one for automobiles, and the top for pedestrians. The lower two slope up from the city's triangle to the bridgeheads across the river; the top is designed level because it is also a planting park. Pedestrians thus walk along a garden over the river.

The bridges are cantilevered off the point by means of a great concrete counterweight, sail-like in form, while cables in equal degrees of tension along the bridge further stabilize the structures. In cross-section, the roadbeds are keel-shaped to provide further stability.

The night rendering depicts the shimmering beauty of the bridges lit against the black skies and reflected on the waters of the rivers below.

44a

BUTTERFLY-WING BRIDGE

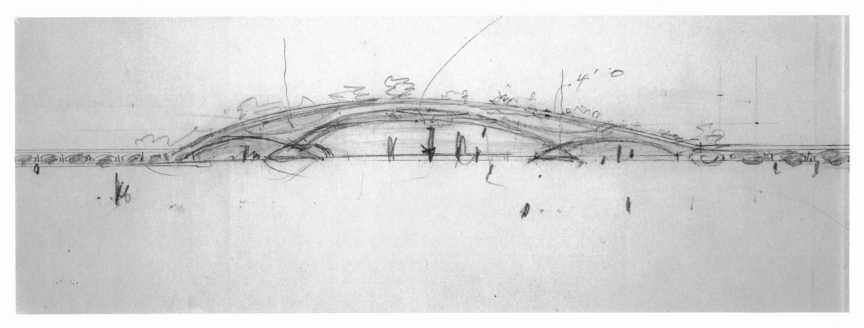

"BUTTERFLY BRIDGE," NEAR SPRING GREEN, WISCONSIN, 1947

The overhead steel-truss bridge, dotted throughout the American landscape, presents a hazard both to human life and to the natural beauty of the terrain. The constant exposure to rain, snow, and frost requires that its steel surfaces be repeatedly painted and repaired to guard against rust. Once a microscopic section of rust sets in, such a bridge is prone to weakening and to eventual collapse.

To provide a safer and better crossing of the Wisconsin River near Taliesin, Mr. Wright designed a new and special kind of bridge. It was to be constructed of poured reinforced concrete, its vital supporting element—steel—thus embedded within the structure, safe from the damaging effects of the elements. He called the structure the Butterfly Bridge (plate 45a) because of the graceful, arched supports that rise up out of the water, spreading like outstretched wings and supporting, in turn, the actual roadbed itself. The parapet of the bridge is a continuation of the arch-support–roadbed system, all poured as one entity for better plasticity, continuity, and strength. The principles at work in this bridge are the same that saved the Imperial Hotel from the ravages of the earthquake in 1923 that took over 100,000 lives and leveled Tokyo and Yokohama.

Referring to the high steel-truss bridges, Mr. Wright once wrote that they "are about as becoming to the landscape as the poles and wires of utility companies—an outrageous imposition pardonable only in a pioneering era. Where civilization has succeeded we have a right to more enlightened consideration."

Shortly after this design was made, the overhead steel-truss bridge that was in use across the river below Taliesin collapsed from the eating-away effect of rust. Three persons died and many more were injured. It was the opportune moment to build this type of bridge. However, small town politics prevailed, as is usual when any element of innovation is presented at government levels. The Butterfly Bridge was not built, though the local citizens for whom it was intended came out strongly in support of it.

In San Francisco two years later, Mr. Wright used this concept of a butterfly-support bridge in designing a bridge for the second crossing of the Southern Bay (plate 45b). Where the bridge needed to rise over a main shipping lane, a great, concrete, thousand-foot span soars up into the sky 175 feet above the water, making it the largest single concrete span in the world. At the apex, the roadbeds separate and give access, if desired, to large discs of concrete that form garden parks that serve as a lookout and a park. The bridge for San Francisco was defeated by the steel lobby, which preferred the traditional exposed steel bridge rather than one of reinforced concrete: the exposed truss type would require a much greater amount of steel than that required for the bridge designed by Mr. Wright.

CRATER RESORT, METEOR CRATER, ARIZONA, 1948

At the edge of a great crater, gouged out of the earth in northern Arizona by the impact of a falling meteor some countless ages ago, Frank Lloyd Wright designed a resort facility with inn, restaurant, shops, and a service station.

When the meteor struck, it displaced a giant area, at the same time creating a swelling at its rim much as if a powerful fist were thrust into a bowl of bread dough. Since the molded slope and the edge are such marked details of the meteor's impact, Mr. Wright incorporated them into the general plan of his building (plate 46). He did not want to level the edge of the crater and thus mar its natural rim or prop the building up on stilts or posts to make all floors on one level. The natural solution, therefore, was to step the building up in a series of terraced levels, a few steps between each, with the roof line sloping smoothly from the lowest to the highest elevation. When the actual rim is reached, in the main lounge and dining areas, the view looks over the bizarre and eerie evidence of some prehistoric touch from another cosmos. A tower at the edge takes tourists up to a higher level for a more extensive view into the crater and also goes down along the inside of the rim until it reaches the bottom. An elevator, called by Mr. Wright an "inclinator," runs down the tower along a diagonal line to gain access to this lower entrance into the very crater itself.

In contrast to the drama that took place ages ago, the proposed building is rather quiet in design. The walls are made of desert masonry, rocks with flat surfaces placed in wooden forms with concrete poured in place until dry. The forms, when removed, reveal a mosaic of varicolored rocks. The roof is covered with cedar-shake shingles stained a natural brown. Thus, the building makes no attempt to compete with the site spread out beneath it. Instead, it encourages a pleasurable communion with the landscape.

Crater Resort was commissioned by Mr. and Mrs. Burton Tremaine who planned in addition a resort lookout containing a museum for exhibiting the various artifacts related to the meteor's strike. For no known reason the Tremaines withdrew the commission.

VINCENT SCULLY HOUSE, WOODBRIDGE, CONNECTICUT, 1948

The house for historian and educator Vincent Scully was designed for a rather narrow, sloping wooded lot near Woodbridge, Connecticut. The plan is a very compact octagon: large living and dining space from the center to one end opening out onto a terrace, the bedrooms wrapping around the living space and extending to the other end of the plan. Below, along with the carport, are provisions for heating, laundry, and storage. The driveway curves around the lot line and descends to the front terrace of the house, which is concealed by the building overhang and by a cluster of trees (plate 47). A complete set of working drawings was finished for this project.

The use of the octagon form for the Scully house is a return, for the first time in more than fifty years, to an architectural shape that Frank Lloyd Wright employed in much of his work before 1900. Many of his earlier houses—McAfee, Husser, Devin, and Cooper—use the full octagon or the half octagon, either as a central unit for the building or as a component feature. In the house for Vincent Scully, the octagonal form is evident but used much more subtly—it is sublimated rather than obvious. The form serves beautifully the need to give interesting spaces to an otherwise small area. Mr. Scully, whom I telephoned while writing this essay, remembers the house design well and commented particularly on its perfect placement in the terrain. The problem was one of money—an eternal one for university professors, it seems. Mr. Wright tried to get the costs down, which could not be done without shrinking the house in a way unacceptable to both architect and client.

Throughout Mr. Wright's career, which began in 1893 and continued until his death in 1959, he always accepted commissions for residential work, though it was his commercial clients' fees that kept his office running. Such has always been the case with architects. There is little profit to be made from designing a private home, and many large architectural firms will not accept residential work. Adler and Sullivan, for whom Mr. Wright worked as chief of design between 1887 and 1893, refused house clients, with some rare exceptions who were mostly personal friends. They turned those jobs over to Mr. Wright.

Frank Lloyd Wright believed so deeply in the importance of designing the moderate-cost home for the American citizen that he never turned a client away simply on the grounds that the work would not net a large fee. He was pleased when he was able to solve the problem of building a beautiful place in which the average client could live. Mr. Wright maintained that there was no such person as the common man. Everyone who came to him for a building was an individual in his eyes, and he created the design for that person which he felt was most appropriate, within the limitations of site and budget.

Occasionally, a client would ask for more and more, unable to really afford it. One time, when Mr. Wright had made several modifications to a plan to suit the client's needs and pocketbook but found himself unable to supply the needs desired for the money provided, he wrote: "My dear Client: Yours seems to be the proverbial case of the champagne appetite accompanied with a beer income. I am afraid that what you want simply can not be had for what you are willing to spend."

SELF-SERVICE GARAGE, PITTSBURGH, PENNSYLVANIA, 1949

Two years after he designed the Pittsburgh Point Park Civic Center projects (plates 43a–d, 44a, 44b), Frank Lloyd Wright was again at work for Edgar J. Kaufmann, Sr., this time to design a large parking garage on a lot next to Kaufmann's department store. The garage would serve not only the store next door but a large segment of Pittsburgh's downtown area, desperately in need of parking space.

The project for Kaufmann was entitled Self-Service Garage. The notion of self-service was then gaining popularity around the country. Markets and drugstores were beginning to use it as means of reducing labor costs and keeping the end product more reasonably priced. In 1949, Mr. Wright created a garage parking system that would be no more difficult to use than parking on the street.

The building (plate 48) ascends in a series of double ramps to a height of six levels, with a basement level for underground parking. The total parking area would accommodate over twelve hundred cars. The center is an open court for ventilation, but the sides facing the streets of the block are closed to prevent strong wind currents during stormy weather or icy blasts in winter. The central court holds a spacious fountain pool to help cool and refresh the air. Smaller pedestrian ramps around the court service the car ramps, and the exterior ramp—the descending exit—is open to the elements on the side but protected from above.

There are two elevators, and the roof parking is combined with planting for greenery and landscaping. The central court contains tall, structural members that rise above the roof in the center to support cables from which the inner edges of the ramps are suspended. The principle of construction is therefore the cantilever, made by reinforced concrete slabs and further stabilized by suspension cables, much like a suspension bridge. The waiting room on the entrance level is a small theater with a curved television screen, designed so that persons who have to wait for someone to come with a car can sit and watch projected TV.

The level that faces Kaufmann's department store contains space for show-windows, with access at the basement level. A closed bridge on the sixth-floor level connects again to Kaufmann's at the office level. But the plan was definitely conceived as a downtown parking facility to serve the entire area.

The project was dropped in 1950, owing to stringent zoning laws. Four years later, the question of a central downtown parking facility again surfaced. Kaufmann asked Mr. Wright once again to submit the drawings for the Self-Service Garage. Accordingly, Mr. Wright got the plans out of the vault at Taliesin and sent them to Kaufmann, reminding him that they (the drawings) were the originals and requesting that he take good care of them and return them to Taliesin.

Over the years, the fate of the parking garage was forgotten, and it was assumed that the preliminary designs had been lost. The loss was especially unfortunate because the spiral had long been a form of great interest to Mr. Wright. Here, the spiral is at its utmost utility; no other form or shape could possibly have solved the problem as well as it did.

A few years ago, we began a search for the Self-Service Garage drawings, writing first to Edgar Kaufmann, Jr., who assured us that the drawings were indeed lost if they were not in the Taliesin archives. He certainly did not have them, nor were they to be found among the papers of his father's estate. A search through the Kauffman / Frank Lloyd Wright correspondence mentioned only that the plans were sent to Kaufmann in 1954. No letter of transmittal marking their return surfaced in the Taliesin files.

Suddenly, not long ago, a research student, looking through some papers of the Pittsburgh Parking Authority, came upon a roll of original Frank Lloyd Wright drawings for a parking structure, signed in 1949. The city of Pittsburgh, assuming ownership of the drawings, planned to give them to the Mellon Library.

At that point Mrs. Wright wrote to the mayor of Pittsburgh, reminding him that an architect's drawings are his instruments of service and rightfully belong to him or to his office. In the case of Mr. Wright's drawings, the Frank Lloyd Wright Foundation is the architect's legal heir.

There was a slight delay while obviously some legal counsel was sought. But soon there came a cordial letter from the mayor, guaranteeing that the drawings would be returned to the archives at Taliesin. Shortly thereafter, the drawings arrived in excellent condition, following an absence of more than thirty years.

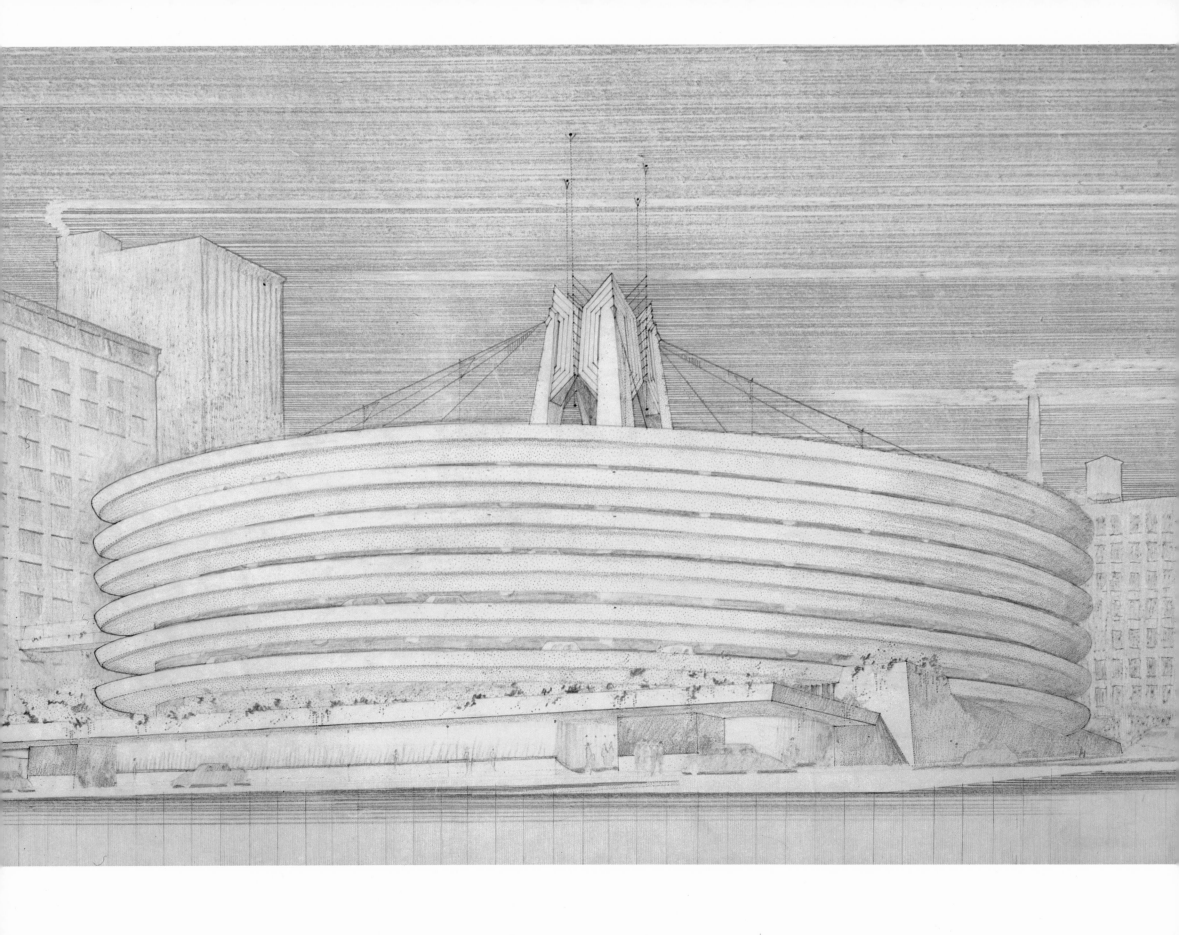

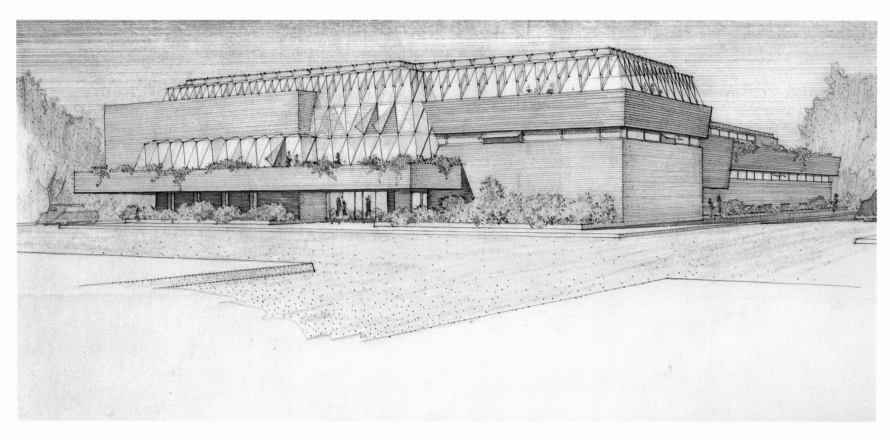

49a

YWCA, RACINE, WISCONSIN, 1949

Herbert F. Johnson, Jr., president of Johnson Wax Company and friend and client of Frank Lloyd Wright, was the moving force behind the selection of Mr. Wright as the architect for a YWCA building in Racine, Wisconsin. He actually paid the architect's fees for the preliminary designs, but the project never went beyond that stage. The YWCA itself was not too enthusiastic about a Frank Lloyd Wright building. Because Johnson's confidence and motivation were not matched by the YWCA's, Mr. Wright felt it unwise to continue a project where the actual clients themselves had not come to him for his work. He made one scheme, then revised it to include a larger project, and eventually dropped it.

But the developed drawings, even though they never reached the working drawing stage, reveal a remarkably detailed and thought-out scheme that could serve as a community center for any smaller American city (plate 49a).

A basement level contains bowling alleys with spectator seating; the entrance level contains a teenage activities room, offices, equipment storage, locker rooms, crafts rooms, administration offices, kitchen, lounge, and gymnasium; the lounge level above contains a dining room, banquet hall extension, kitchen, music rooms, club rooms, office for directors, and the upper part of the gymnasium with spectators' gallery and dressing rooms; the top level contains a swimming pool under a glass canopy, locker rooms, dressing rooms, swimming lounge, and a roof garden for sun bathing.

An airy court (plate 49b) planted with tropical plants and covered with a skylight above serves all the levels. Ramps connect the various levels, along with provisions for elevators and stairs. The project contained everything that could possibly be needed for a structure of this kind, including innovative elegance.

49b

**GOETSCH-WINCKLER HOUSE NUMBER TWO
OKEMOS, MICHIGAN, 1949**

Alma Goetsch and Katherine Winckler were two teachers who had built one of the first Usonian (moderate-cost) houses in Okemos, Michigan, in 1939. Their home was to be part of a group of seven houses for seven teachers at the state university, planned as a total community and called Usonia I, Lansing, Michigan. Although each of the houses was an individual plan, the system of construction—board and batten walls set on a concrete mat with the masonry masses composed of brick—was the same for them all. This was in the era when carpentry labor was relatively inexpensive. Once the method of making the sandwich walls was understood, then having them factory-made for other houses would reduce the overall costs. The same applied to the other trades: concrete masonry, masonry, electrical, plumbing, and so forth. In short, the project was intended to bring the factory to the site, rather than the skilled laborer.

When the other clients took their drawings to the local banks for loans, they were told that such a house would have no resale value, that the open space was undesirable, that kitchens should be separate rooms rather than alcoves adjacent to the dining tables, that the "style" was not appropriate for college faculty houses. They were denied help and forced to choose another architect. But because Miss Goetsch and Miss Winckler could combine their salaries, they were able to finance their home.

The Goetsch-Winckler house is small, simple, and inexpensive, yet it immediately became famous and was published here and abroad. It demonstrated what one of the world's greatest architects could do when the budget was extremely limited. It was a distinctly individual house, American in character, built in a time when small houses were usually Colonial boxes.

Years later, Miss Goetsch and Miss Winckler came back to Mr. Wright for the design of a larger house, also to be built in Okemos. The budget this time was considerably larger. The plan designed by Mr. Wright (plate 50) provided for an entry loggia in the center, a large living and dining area on one side, and a bedroom wing running out at a 120-degree angle and ending with a studio. The working drawings specified standard 8" x 16" concrete block, though the presentation drawings showed brick. This was frequently the case. When the originally recommended masonry material was too expensive, Mr. Wright would then change the material to a less costly one.

His method of laying up the concrete blocks was to rake the horizontal joint, so as to give a shadow line, a deep reveal, to accentuate the horizontal quality of the masonry, while the vertical joint was brought up flush with the block surface so as to minimize the vertical lines between the blocks. He often stepped the block courses as they rose, either 3/8" in or out per course. This gives a sculptural quality to the masonry achieved by means of shadow lines. Taking a common material and giving it great poetry was but one aspect of his genius.

The second Goetsch-Winckler house would have been superb, as the drawing attests. However, budget considerations became insurmountable and the project was not built.

SENATOR GEORGE GRISWOLD HOUSE, GREENWICH, CONNECTICUT, 1949

Although this project, designed for Connecticut Senator George Griswold, is quite large, the sense of interior space never projects megalomania as it so easily could in any mansion-scale residence. The various areas within the main space are larger and more elaborately planned than they would be for a

house of more moderate cost, yet space still flows from area to area in human scale. The section taken through the living room and out onto the ocean-side terrace shows the scale and flow within the building (plate 51).

The drama of the interior and its relationship to the view is enhanced by the plan, which permits the view to be seen in stages rather than in direct confrontation. It is the same principle at work that he used in the plan of the Booth house (plate 5) in its wooded glen. By limiting the view, by concentrating it, and by directing it with care and good planning, the view becomes that much more exciting. In the Griswold plan, the owner can look out from his own private balcony along the coastline. Or he can look over the balcony from his bedroom through the tall glass doors that lead directly to a view of the ocean. Seeing the water mainly in reference to the inside of the house blends the interior with the ocean's edge and beyond.

Here is an example of a limitation being a best friend. Great natural conditions, in this case the ocean, can be incorporated into the very life of the interior of the building. The exterior thus maintains a constant point of reference to that which is within. It is an oriental way of thinking, an oriental approach to life. We of the West are accustomed to the straight line; the orientals think in terms of the spiral line. Mr. Wright's nature observed and comprehended both the East and the West, which gave a dimension and a meaning to his work. It is this beautiful blend of the direct, straightforward Western approach with the curvilinear, contemplative Eastern way of thought that gives such richness and fullness to the Griswold project and to so much of the work of Frank Lloyd Wright.

"CROWNFIELD," ROBERT F. WINDFOHR HOUSE, FORT WORTH, TEXAS, 1949

Robert and Ann Windfohr, Texans from Fort Worth, came to Mr. Wright in February 1949, wishing a luxury home on the wide prairie at the outskirts of their city. In a very short period of time, Mr. Wright prepared the sketches for the home he called "Crownfield," focusing it around a large circular living room (plate 52). Out from this circle, which contained separate inner circles for fireplace gatherings, music, and dancing, were the other two major wings of the house. One contained a formal dining room, with its own conservatory, breakfast rooms, and cardrooms for games, that ended in a wing for food preparation and servants' dwellings. On the other side, at a 120-degree angle, extended the master bedroom and guest room areas, occupying two floors.

The general character of the poured concrete residence is represented by softly curved walls with circular windows, a dome with glass tubing over the central living room, and curved roofs over the remaining structure.

The plans never went beyond the preliminary stage. The Windfohrs vacillated, kept the drawings for a long time before returning them, suggested some changes (which was usually the case and usually what Mr. Wright expected), and then, without any legitimate explanation, let the scheme die. Mr. Wright tried several times to reach them to discover what stage the project was in, why they were reluctant. No word.

Finally, Mr. Wright put away the drawings. Three years later he took out the scheme and redeveloped it for the Mexican cabinet minister, Raul Bailleres (plates 53a, 53b). It was to fail again, only to be presented for a third time, again modified and redeveloped, for Marilyn Monroe in 1957 (plates 66a, 66b). However, this exceptionally grand and elegant home was destined never to be built. Some beautiful works seem fated to remain only projects.

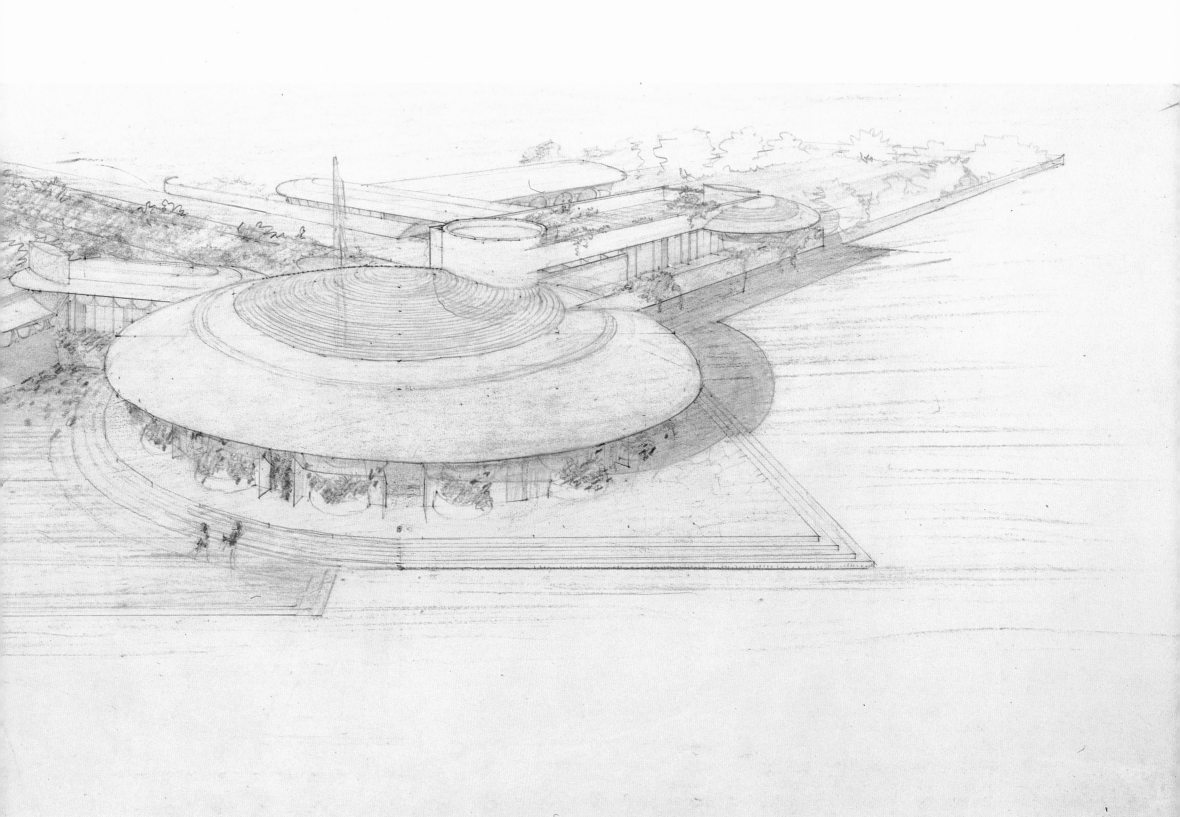

Raul Bailleres, a cabinet minister in the Mexican government, was a man of considerable wealth, great charm, and cultivation. He saw Frank Lloyd Wright's work in an exhibition in Mexico City and invited the architect to come to Mexico and view a building site he had purchased in Acapulco. Mr. Wright visited the cliff-side property with its luxuriant foliage and its terrain covered with large, natural boulders. From a boat along the coastline he studied the drama of the land and its relation to the bay.

Bailleres commissioned a luxury vacation home for the Acapulco site. When Mr. Wright returned to Taliesin, he brought out the drawings for the Windfohr house (plate 52) and began to redesign the work. Once conceived for a Texas prairie, it was now to be made appropriate for the Mexican coastline. The proximity of the sea below, the cliffs, the prolific scattering of beautiful boulders all inspired Mr. Wright to design a home in and around the on-site boulders above the sea, with ramps and walkways going down to the ocean edge below (plates 53a, 53b).

The quality of an open-air summer home is preserved in the generous forms of circles and domes, curved roof lines, and full-circle and half-circle windows. The dining room, adjacent to the main circle patio, contains an orchid conservatory running along one side. Wings extend out from the main residence for servants, guests, stables, garages, and a caretaker's house. The fireplaces in the earlier house are converted to indoor fountains for this tropical region so perfectly suited to the sound of gently cascading jets of water.

Everything about the design of the Bailleres house suggests gracious living in a tropical setting—above the ocean but connected to it. Shortly after the preliminary drawings were made and sent to the Bailleres family, the death of their young son in an automobile accident extinguished their desire to build the home. It was a tragedy that, combined with a sudden change of political scene, affected the senior Bailleres permanently. The drawings were returned to the architect, and the house remains unbuilt.

RAUL BAILLERES HOUSE, ACAPULCO, MEXICO, 1952

53a

53b

V A T I O N   S O U T H W E S T   E L E V A T I O N

Mr. Wright designed three fraternity houses during his career, in 1924, 1941, and the Zeta Beta Tau Fraternity House in 1952. None was ever built. Although each of the three differed from the others in materials employed, site, and location, one design feature was common to all three. Each contained a large two or three-story living room to serve as a great hall at one end of the building, with dormitory bedrooms stretching out behind it. In the case of the Zeta Beta Tau House, the great hall gives onto a large circular outdoor terrace for dining and entertainment (plate 54).

The project progressed as far as the working drawing stage, but the clients were a committee—a deadly situation especially where creative work is concerned. A committee, Mr. Wright once said, functions like a jury selection. First they throw out the worst; then they throw out the best; then they settle on the middle ground as being the safest. The factor of safety, Dankmar Adler once insisted, becomes frequently a factor of ignorance. How often it was that much that is the best of Mr. Wright's work was not built simply because of this factor.

When the Frank Lloyd Wright Foundation was required, many years ago, to pay certain back taxes accrued by the late Mr. Wright, the Foundation met the payment largely by means of architectural commissions still coming into the office at that time.

"You have three things," Mr. Wright told his wife, "to protect you and Taliesin in times of need: the oriental art collections, the land in Wisconsin, and my architectural drawings." Banker Walter Bimson dined with Mrs. Wright at Taliesin one evening after the tax case had been settled and the payments met. "Don't you feel regretful, Olgivanna," he asked, "that you had to give all that money to the U.S. Government after Frank's death?" "No, Walter. Do you realize that the United States of America is the *only* nation in the world where Frank could have designed and built what he did? In a way this is his great debt, now finally paid, to the country he so intensely loved."

POINT VIEW RESIDENCES
PITTSBURGH, PENNSYLVANIA, 1952

When Edgar J. Kaufmann, Sr., the client for whom Frank Lloyd Wright built Fallingwater, asked Mr. Wright to design an apartment building in Pittsburgh, the architect turned to one of his unexecuted designs of 1929, a small apartment building for Elizabeth Noble of Los Angeles. From the smaller scheme, Mr. Wright developed his plan for the Pittsburgh apartments. The fenestration of the building is one of its outstanding features. Rather than a single corner, the corner is stepped back in a series of receding angles. It thus becomes more varied, more crystalline.

Each of the apartments is set one-half level above the one next to it. In this way, sound does not travel through the structural beams and slabs. Each level is one self-contained apartment, with privacy guaranteed to a degree never before achieved. The project was developed to the working drawing stage, the drawings signed and delivered and the specifications completed, when suddenly Mr. Wright withdrew the work and prepared an entirely different design.

Frank Lloyd Wright sought continually to improve his work. There were times when he would take a drawing made by him many years previously and alter it extensively. Frequently, this was for his own clarification. He would take part of a work that was already designed and built, then use the drawings to make marginal notes as a form of elucidation and explanation. He regarded his collection of drawings as a personal and historic library. Notes abound on many of them, written years after their first creation.

He sought as well to improve his own home and work buildings, and he applied this same principle to work already done for his clients. Nothing stood in his way when he saw the necessity for change. Change was a constant companion in his life; it was one of the factors that kept him young.

Thus, after he had signed the complete set of working drawings for the Point View Residences, he sat down one day and took out the first sheet—the plot plan—showing the contours of the steep hillslope. The drawing was beautifully done in pencil and ink based on a unit system drawn in thin, precise red lines. In itself, the working drawing was a work of art, chiseled, clear, expertly drawn. However, it was still mainly a revision of the Elizabeth Noble Apartments of 1929. On the other hand, he had never used the form of a triangle for a tall structure. Other towers he had designed were square, like Rogers Lacy (plates 36a–c), or combined square and circle, like the Johnson Research Laboratory, or the more conventional rectangle, like the Press Building and the National Life Insurance Building (plate 12).

For the Point View Residences he went back to the drafting room, and on the first sheet of the working drawings set made the preliminary studies for a triangular apartment tower (plates 55a, 55b). Each floor is one, large, three-thousand-square-foot apartment, with terraces and balconies facing in all three directions. The areas adjacent to the roadbed provide garage and storage facilities. The apartments are spacious, with large rooms each offering expansive views. As in most of Mr. Wright's designs for tall buildings out in the sunlight, copper louvers protect the glass with visors, which screen off the direct rays of the sun but retain the views unimpeded.

Unfortunately, when Kaufmann consulted several developers about the property chosen for the Point View Residences, they cautioned against putting up an apartment building on that particular site, especially a building intended for retired senior citizens. The area was beautiful and offered a commanding view of the river below and Pittsburgh beyond. However, it was isolated—the families who would rent or purchase the apartments would find no stores, shops, or commercial areas nearby. At that time, there was no shopping within walking distance. The residents would have to drive to get their simple everyday needs, or else go by taxi. Over and over again Kaufmann tried to convince the developers that the area would grow, would prosper and be able to support the type of local shops necessary to make the apartment building work. But each time he came up against a blank wall, and when he went to marketing experts he was assured once again that the site was too remote. With the odds thus stacked against him, he felt it best to abandon the project.

If Venice had built this chastely romantic student dwelling, it would have had on its historic Grand Canal a twentieth-century structure in perfect keeping with Venetian Renaissance tradition (plate 56).

Pioneer of modern architecture though he was, Mr. Wright had a great respect for tradition. When he was in Tokyo making his designs for the Imperial Hotel, he discarded the design he had made in Chicago in 1914 in favor of a new one, more, he said, in harmony with the essential mood of Japan. "There was a great tradition there worthy of respect and I felt it my duty as well as my privilege to make the building belong to them so far as I might."

He felt the same way about Venice, a city dear to his heart. When his exhibit Sixty Years of Living Architecture toured Europe in 1951, he journeyed to Venice where he received the Star of Solidarity, Italy's highest honor, in the Ducal Palace. The entire affair with its resplendent medieval trappings was very moving and made a deep impression on him.

While in Venice at that time, he met a young architect, Angelo Masieri. Two years later, Masieri and his wife traveled to the United States and motored across country to Wisconsin to pay their respects to Mr. Wright at Taliesin. On their return they were involved in an automobile accident on the Pennsylvania turnpike. The young architect was killed, but his wife, Savina Masieri, survived.

From her native Venice she wrote to Mr. Wright about the accident, the death of her husband, and her intention to honor him by erecting a building of Mr. Wright's design on the Grand Canal in Venice. Their family owned a piece of property on the canal, and it was their intention to construct a notable dwelling for architectural students. Mr. Wright accepted the commission, and in a very short time the building was designed and the preliminaries sent to Venice.

As soon as it was known that Frank Lloyd Wright had designed a building for Venice, a great controversy erupted over the construction of a modern building in ancient Venice. The Venetian officials, having seen the drawings, were delighted with the work, but the tourist agencies feared that something new would "ruin" the atmosphere of the city. At one point Ernest Hemingway, then living in Africa but a noted champion of Venice, was asked what he thought about a Frank Lloyd Wright building lodged on the Grand Canal. Hemingway said that he would rather see Venice burn then erect a Frank Lloyd Wright building. The press called Mr. Wright to ask his reaction to Hemingway's remark: "Reaction? Why none, whatsoever. After all, that was nothing more than a mere voice from the jungle."

But the controversy raged on, and Mr. Wright composed the following reply, which he called "This Venice Affair."

Venice is unique—a treasure for the whole world. Venice should not die just to please the tourist or sentimental painter. Architecture should keep alive what is most worth preserving in Venice, and that means to cut away what is already unfit to live, if Venice is to live as herself. In this salvage, better building from the bottom up is needed. But no need to lose or damage her native beauty. The problem is one for an architect knowing scientific construction, and understanding what constitutes the true beauty of Venice, to preserve what made her as beautiful as she is. The progress the art of building has already made should now serve to preserve her.

Planning construction for Venice is like planning construction for any city or situation where the unique character of a culture prevails. This requires love from, and love for, the true artist. Architecture is the art that should rescue, not destroy.

Venice does not float upon the water like a gondola, but rests upon the silt at the bottom of the sea. In the little building I have designed, slender marble shafts firmly fixed upon concrete piles (two to each) in the silt rise from the water as do reeds or rice or any water plants. These marble piers rise to carry the floor construction securely— the cantilever slab floors thus made safe to project between balconies overhanging the water—Venetian as Venetian can be. Not imitation, but interpretation of Venice. Frank Lloyd Wright, Taliesin West, Phoenix, Arizona, March 24th, 1954.

But pressure from the tourist agencies, against the scheme from the outset, was too great for the Venetian city fathers to oppose. A tourist city by nature, she derived the greater part of her living from the tourist agencies' pipeline. The project was dropped.

56

57

YOSEMITE NATIONAL PARK RESTAURANT, YOSEMITE, CALIFORNIA, 1953

This project, a restaurant providing for dining indoors as well as on a great circular terrace looking up at the canyon walls at Yosemite National Park, was rejected on the grounds that it was not "rustic." In short, the design did not make use of the typical logs and fieldstones that, according to the authorities, tourists have come to associate with the buildings placed in our national parks.

Although the official explanation for the refusal of Mr. Wright's design placed the blame on the conservative element involved, in reality the project was dropped for purely political reasons. The client, a firm called Degnan-Donahoe, had held the franchise for restaurants in the Yosemite valley for a long time. Then a new and large organization wanted to take over the concession and got the head of the park service to vote out the Frank Lloyd Wright design on the trumped-up charge that it would "compete with the natural beauty of the park."

Just the opposite is the case (plate 57). The profile of the building is low and gentle, emphasizing a simple form that would adapt to, not compete with, the natural drama of the cliffs, forest, and waterfalls.

"SEA CLIFF," V. C. MORRIS HOUSE (SCHEME TWO) SAN FRANCISCO, CALIFORNIA, 1954

Although Frank Lloyd Wright was born in the Midwest and lived during most of his life in Wisconsin and in Arizona, the residences he designed to be built on the edge of the sea reflect his love for it. He had his own particular ways of bringing the seascape right into the life of the people whose houses he designed for the ocean's edge. Sometimes the structure affords an extended horizontal outlook over the ocean, as in the houses he designed

for John Nesbitt in Carmel, California (plate 23a), and for Senator Griswold in Connecticut (plate 51). With the Haldorn residence, also in Carmel, the home is placed back from the sea in secluded circles around a garden court, a roof garden covering the entire structure. The living area is central to the plan, with all window areas for the view of the nearby ocean. For the painter Franklin Watkins he designed a small cottage-studio (plate 26) set into sand dunes on the New Jersey coastline, with the required north light for a painter, but with sun decks all around to take advantage of the sea's presence. By far the most dramatic seaside home he created was the house he called Sea Cliff for V. C. Morris in San Francisco Bay (plate 34).

The construction of Sea Cliff was postponed by the Morrises in 1945. Almost ten years later, however, they asked Mr. Wright to prepare another set of working drawings for a new design to be built on the same site (plate 58).

It was becoming a repetitive situation. Instead of going ahead and building the house that they had always wanted on the property that they loved, Mr. and Mrs. Morris were again "going to shore to pick up more wood so as to build up more steam for the trip."

Mr. Morris's sudden death curtailed the plans to build. Mrs. Morris did not want to go ahead on that particular property now that she was alone. Mr. Wright, sympathetic, advised her to keep the property as an investment, since it was growing in value every day. He also suggested she find something quieter and less dramatic for herself, something that would require a simpler design. She took his advice and purchased a flat beach site at Stinson Beach, still in the San Francisco Bay area. "Quietwater" was a low, sheltered house that Mr. Wright designed for her on that beach, but by the time the working drawings were finished and signed, she too had died.

Vienna-born Max Hoffmann had been a racing-car driver before World War II. His business acumen bordered on sheer genius, and when the war was over he went to the Jaguar people in England and convinced them that a small sport racing car such as their XK-120 was bound to be a success in the United States. He further convinced them to give him the exclusive American franchise for all U.S. Jaguar imports.

He set himself up in business on New York's elegant Park Avenue and commissioned Frank Lloyd Wright to design an automobile showroom at number 430. Part of the design of the showroom included a large turntable in the center with three shining cars on it, a mirror for its floor, and another mirror on the ceiling. In a planting area nearby was planned a statue of the jaguar itself, to be made in Coventry, England. The jaguar was shown as it appears on the automobile's hood ornament. Frozen in space in a great outstretched leap, it measured nearly ten feet from the tip of the nose to the tail.

The Jaguar had enjoyed tremendous sales, largely owing to Hoffmann's insight, but the company began to resent the power that Hoffmann wielded. Every car that came into the United States had to come through his jurisdiction. Jaguar decided to buy out the Hoffmann franchise for the sum of $7 million. Hoffmann immediately invested in Mercedes-Benz and took over that franchise in place of the Jaguar. Just as the transfer was under way, the statue of the jaguar arrived. Hoffmann came on the scene and saw the statue. He was short and rather heavy set, imperious, and spoke with a heavy Viennese accent. "Take it away, take it out, get rid of it!" He shouted as he strode out the door.

Hoffmann also commissioned Mr. Wright to design a home near Rye, New York. Mr. Wright made several trips to the building site with Hoffmann driving a small Porsche like the racing car driver he had once been. The architect enjoyed the trips, admiring the dexterous way in which Hoffmann quickly wove in and out of traffic.

Mr. Wright loved foreign cars and collected them himself; including, with the discount from Hoffmann, a Jaguar Mark IV, Mark V, and Mark VII. When Hoffmann changed midstream from Jaguar to Mercedes, Mr. Wright bought a beautiful Mercedes touring car. He admired the scale of European cars and said that an automobile should resemble a fish in design rather than the overbuilt shoe-box type currently manufactured in the United States.

Mr. Wright made Hoffmann's house design fit the business stature of his client (plate 59). The structure is vast and grand, with a tall, cathedral-like living room. Hoffmann was a short man whose principal outlet was automobiles. He found the design too overpowering, exclaiming when he saw it, "But it is too big for me, Mr. Wright! Just too big!"

The home that Mr. Wright finally built for him is different, still beautiful but closer to the scale that his client desired. It is an extremely well built, impressive house looking out over the sound. The original version would have been a more splendid example, however, of elegant living on a grand scale.

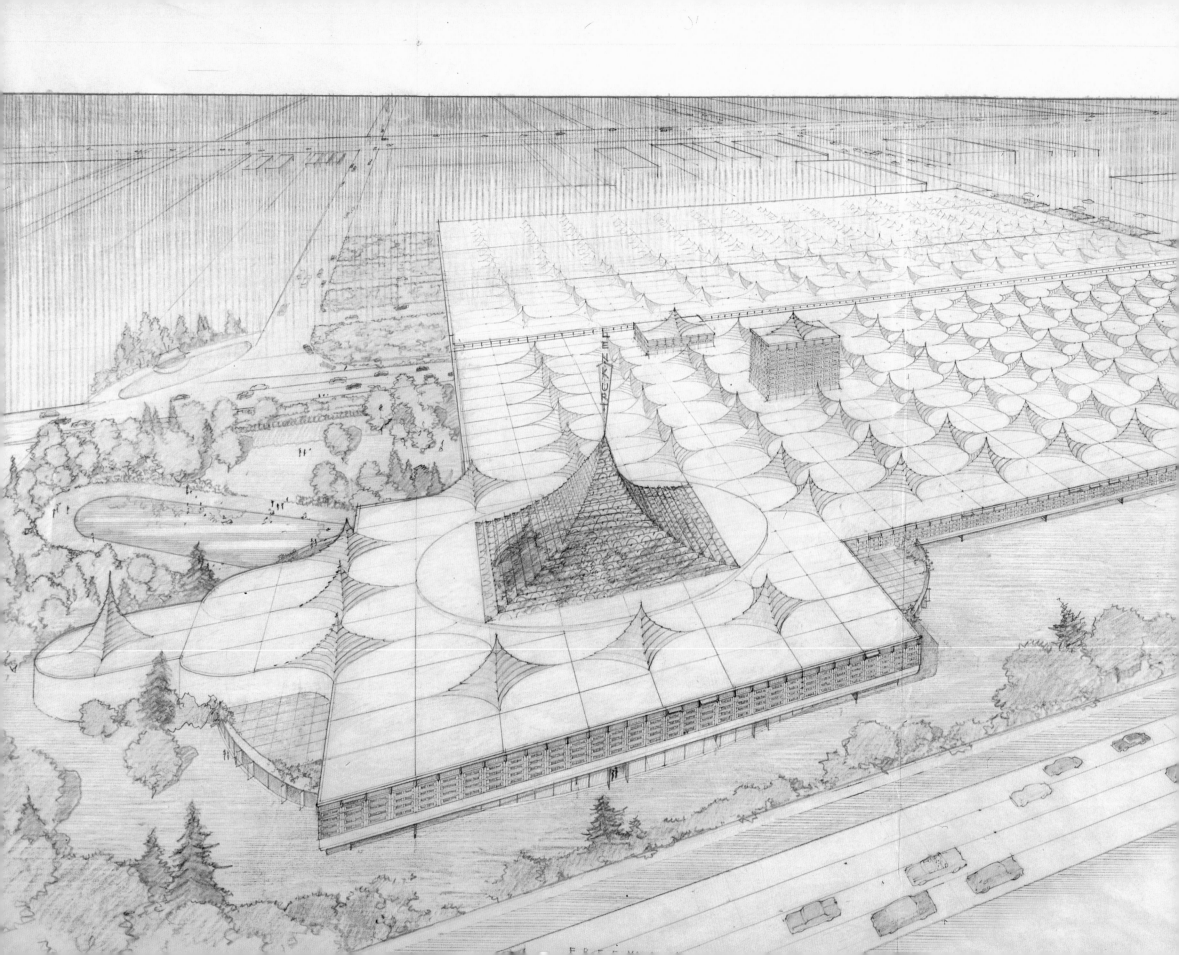

LENKURT ELECTRIC COMPANY, SAN MATEO, CALIFORNIA, 1955

The Lenkurt Electric Company was founded by two Californians, Lennart Erickson and Kurt Appert, whose combined names gave the firm its own name. The company manufactured microwave and telephone systems, and it had grown to become a sizeable corporation by 1955. Totally owned and controlled by Erickson and Appert, it was based in San Mateo, California. In 1955, when the two men decided that they wanted a new industrial plant, they came to Taliesin to confer with Frank Lloyd Wright.

When Mr. Wright was revising the Lenkurt working drawings the year after he made his first sketches, he wrote an explanation to the executives: "I hope you will all like the work as much as we do. And I believe a remarkably fine thing is going to be your contribution to American culture. The business world can do most after the American dwelling. . . . I hope the company will not consider the episode closed to changes that may occur after the plans have been made or during their preparation. The whole project is such that great flexibility is possible without damage to the original idea—so do not worry about dotting the i's and crossing the t's."

Every mechanical advantage comes equipped, it seems, with its own built-in drawback, sometimes even with its own curse. The automobile is certainly a case in point. Whenever a considerable amount of people are congregated together, a parking problem arises, particularly during civic, cultural, or athletic events. Also, with industries employing many workers the problem becomes quickly one of gigantic proportions. Avoiding this nightmare, both the discomfort and the ugliness spread out and around fine architecture, was a prime consideration in Mr. Wright's mind when he designed large projects such as the Pittsburgh Point Civic Center (plates 43a–d, 44a, 44b). It was also paramount in his thinking about the Lenkurt factory. Lenkurt Electric could have been turned into a conventional industrial site surrounded by an

60a

ocean of parked cars baking in the California sunshine. Such is not the case with this design (plate 60a). The entire ground level is taken over by parking, shaded and protected, with each area having access by means of stairs, ramps, and elevators to the working area above. The employees thus park their cars directly under the place where they work. The column supports for the factory are based on the same dendriform columns that were so successful in the Johnson Administration Building. In that work, the columns rise to support floors, and in turn become the roof, forming large pads of circles above. Where the circular pads meet, a flat glass-tube skylight was used in the Johnson Building. But in Lenkurt (plate 60c), pagoda-like skylights rise up above the roofline, made of glass with copper louvers, to control the amount of daylight desired at any one time.

The plan is a unit system of component parts making up the whole building. The project can be expanded as needed. On one corner, a large, airy, three-story pavilion contains an auditorium for films and lectures, and a cafe under a great copper and glass dome sheltering ample gardens and lagoons. Offices for executives (plate 60b) are on the balcony level of this pavilion, with views both into the inner court and of the outdoors.

The total accomplishment was a beautiful industrial building designed to be built out in the countryside and bordering a lagoon near San Mateo (plate 60d). But by the time that the working drawings were finished and the Lenkurt owners were ready to negotiate with contractors, Western Electric offered to buy them out. The price was so handsome that they accepted, sold their company, and returned the plans to Mr. Wright at Taliesin.

60d

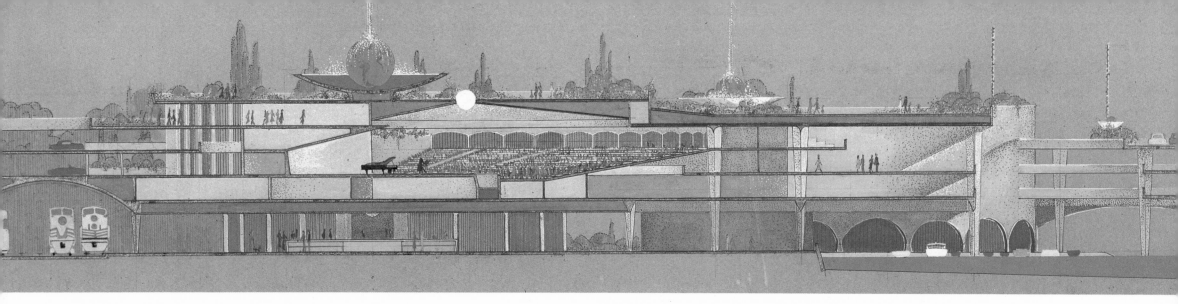

MONONA TERRACE CIVIC CENTER (SCHEME TWO)
MADISON, WISCONSIN, 1955

The Monona Terrace Civic Center as first proposed in 1938 (plates 22a, 22b) dropped into oblivion and then surfaced again in 1955—but not at the instigation of municipal government or authority. Wisconsin scholar Mary Jane Hamilton has researched this long-time project and found that it was never a civic project. The city and the politicians involved always had other sites in mind and other architects at work on the idea of a civic center. In both instances of Mr. Wright's involvement, scheme one and scheme two were brought alive by the concentrated effort of private individuals who wanted Madison to have something more than another commonplace building.

Following the Second World War, the citizens of Madison again took up the problem of not having a civic center. Culturally, the state's capital was taking a back seat to thriving Milwaukee, some seventy miles away. This time, four people began to devote all their time and energy to getting the people of Madison interested in the Monona Terrace Project—Professor Harold Groves and his wife Helen and Professor Don Lescohier and his wife Mary. Another staunch supporter of the project was William T. Evjue, the editor and publisher of the *Capital Times*. He offered his newspaper's front page time and time again for this crusade.

The Groves and the Lescohiers were members of the First Unitarian Society of Madison. Beginning in 1946, they were among the members of the congregation most instrumental in getting Frank Lloyd Wright as the architect for their new church building. By 1949, the church was under construction, but in 1951 they ran out of building funds. The church was roofed and nearly finished except for interior details and the final touches—painting, plastering, and furnishings. It looked as though the building was going to remain in that unfinished state when Mr. Wright decided that he would come in with the Taliesin Fellowship and finish the building for them. Each day that summer we drove forty miles, breakfasted at a small diner near the construction site, and worked the rest of the day. By the summer's end, the church was completed and dedicated. Some thirty years later, it was designated by the American Institute of Architects as one of America's buildings worthy of permanent preservation.

For reasons such as these, the Monona project became an issue of great fervor and intensity. Mr. Wright's friend Bill Evjue fought for the building through his newspaper with a passion that resembled a political crusade. To some extent, this constant support and praise for the Terrace on the front page of the daily newspapers helped to defeat it. The people of Madison saw this project as a political football, which Mr. Wright had predicted as early as 1938. The almost daily arguments and controversies began to turn into tirades and insults between politicians. The very words "Monona Terrace" became a red flag, and constant publicity began to irritate the citizens of Madison.

Helen Groves and Mary Lescohier did their utmost to turn the tide. Mr. Wright prepared a revised set of preliminary drawings (plates 61a, 61b) and explained the new revisions through the use of a large model that was widely exhibited. A petition was circulated throughout Madison calling for a referendum. The people voted for the center and for the appropriation of funds to build it. Politics and personal prejudice again rose up and defeated the very thing the people desired and were willing to support by municipal bonds.

The center was defeated, for the time being, until a new mayor, Ivan Nestingen, came forward in favor of the project. Had he remained in office, Monona Terrace would unquestionably have been built. He was appointed by President Kennedy to the post of Secretary for Health, Education, and Welfare. He resigned as mayor, moved to Washington, and the Terrace was irrevocably consigned to the drawing board.

Mr. Wright had long considered the Monona Terrace a lost cause for the city of Madison. He never ceased to admire the persistence and dedication of Helen Groves and Mary Lescohier. Whenever they rallied to the cause he instantly supported them and took time to consult with them. A voluminous correspondence went on between them on behalf of the Terrace long after it was generally recognized that such crusading would only prove fruitless.

In the last decade of Frank Lloyd Wright's life, many requests came from clients desiring houses for low or moderate budgets. It was impossible to fulfill these requests in terms of a custom-designed house. Therefore, after 1950, Mr. Wright began responding that he was at work on a low-cost housing design called the Usonian Automatic. As early as 1949 he began putting ideas for the Usonian Automatic down on paper.

Basically, Mr. Wright believed that the middle-income client, wherever and whenever possible, should become actively involved in building the home, should try to keep skilled labor off the site as much as possible, and should contract separately for plumbing, electrical, and other specialist trades. As for the general construction of the house, that could be achieved by simpler, cheaper labor. The four concrete block houses of California in 1923 for Millard, Freeman, Storer, and Ennis had revolutionized the concept of the concrete block. These magically beautiful houses all achieved great beauty by means of what was then generally considered the basest building material on the market. In the hands of a genius, this once-despised material, the lowly concrete block, took on poetry and produced a result that continues to amaze and delight. With a simple artistic adaptation, the block becomes a woven tapestry of lovely forms and shapes, playing with sunlight and shadows. The wall surfaces are delicate screens of pattern that never cease to please the eye, creating what Mr. Wright loved to call eye-music, something as rhythmic and melodic to look at as a beautiful symphony is to listen to.

Concrete blocks (plate 62a) were designed to be made of thin shells of concrete, with half-circular grooves running around the four edges. Blocks placed next to each other, and placed one course over the other, thus formed circular cavities within for the placement of thin steel rods, about the thickness of a pencil. As the courses of block rose, concrete grout or mortar was poured into those cavities, binding the wall blocks and reinforcing rods into one monolithic structure. The great expense of skilled masons laying courses of blocks with exposed mortar joints was thus circumvented.

With this new development of block construction, the Usonian Automatic became feasible as well as interesting and attractive. (*Usonia* was British author Samuel Butler's name for America. *Automatic* designates the capability of the average client to build his own home.) Houses like the Usonian Automatic for Gerald Sussman (plate 62b) were finally under construction by 1953. The first one was built for Benjamin Adelman near the Arizona Biltmore Hotel in Phoenix, the second one for Gerald Tonkens in Ohio.

In the Sussman prototype, the concrete blocks are designed so that the client could build an outer shell and add a second, more insulated wall later if desired. The ceiling was also composed of blocks set up on a wooden form, steel reinforcing rods tied into the blocks and then the whole poured in place. The result is a monolithic structure—slabs, walls, and roof—that is fireproof and earthquake-proof. No color, painting, or surfacing would be required for the blocks; no maintenance or repainting would be necessary. Electrical and plumbing systems were to be modular and prefabricated. Furniture of special design was to be made out of plywood on the site or in a shop on a mass-produced basis, should many Automatics be in construction in one area.

Intriguing as it was, the Sussman house was never built. So much work was coming into the studio at that time, however, that the reason for the loss of a small project like this one was never chronicled.

The Usonian system could still work well on a nationwide scale, if the blocks and the component systems were mass produced. Such a system would solve beautifully the problem of a moderately low-cost house for the great number of persons seeking individuality with economy.

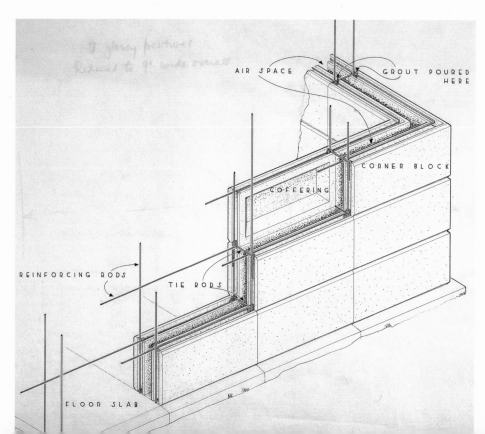

62a

62b

CHRISTIAN SCIENCE CHURCH, BOLINAS, CALIFORNIA, 1956

During his career, Frank Lloyd Wright designed twenty religious buildings, including churches, chapels, temples, and a synagogue. Of these, eight were built for diverse faiths and under diverse conditions. Mr. Wright utilized in each case the form that best expressed that particular faith. Unity Temple in Oak Park is housed in a square to signify unity, strength, and oneness. The Greek Orthodox church in Milwaukee takes the Greek Cross and the dome as its two inspiring forms, and upon that thesis the entire edifice is designed. The Unitarian Church in Madison, Wisconsin, is based on the shape of the triangle—aspiration—and places the minister at the apex of the triangle with his congregation spread out before him under a great sloping ceiling that is roof and steeple in one. "No more the pointing finger to heaven," Mr. Wright said. "The old traditional steeple is now eliminated in favor of a generous protecting roof rising up like the attitude of two hands clasped in prayer."

Mr. Wright was never narrow-minded or prejudiced in his outlook on life, be it his own or the lives of others around him. He was expansive and receptive to ideas. He deeply admired variety, in nature and in point of view, and he relished the complex variety of the human species. He was highly ethical, and he had profound faith in the sovereignty of the individual. As he upheld the individual, he deplored the masses. He interpreted democracy as the doctrine of the individual and communism as the doctrine of the masses. In any religious building that he created, the architect grasped the essential nature of that particular sectarian application of the one great Idea he called God and made the building expressive of that Idea. "Love of God is Love of an Idea," he once said, and his widow had that statement placed on his gravestone.

These principles of design and creation he employed for the relatively small church set at the edge of a forest on a grass plain for the Christian Scientists in Bolinas, California, in 1956. The plan for this church (plate 63) is purposefully simple: a square containing a circle within, the roof a flat plane; the window walls on three sides a curve sweeping down from each corner to the center then back up again; and full-length glass doors on the entry side. There is no darkness, no mystery, no cavernous vast interior spaces to force humans to their knees in fear and supplication. On the contrary, this church speaks directly of clear trust and faith in pure thought.

The committee that approached Mr. Wright to design this church was led by one of the "Silver Barons" of San Francisco, Herford Sharon. He and his wife were the motivating force that moved this project from its conception stages up through the finished working drawings. But the ensuing power play that often occurs in committees began to work against the fulfillment of the design. The other committee members resented the preeminence of the Sharon family, and they were finally forced to step down, whereupon the building project was abandoned.

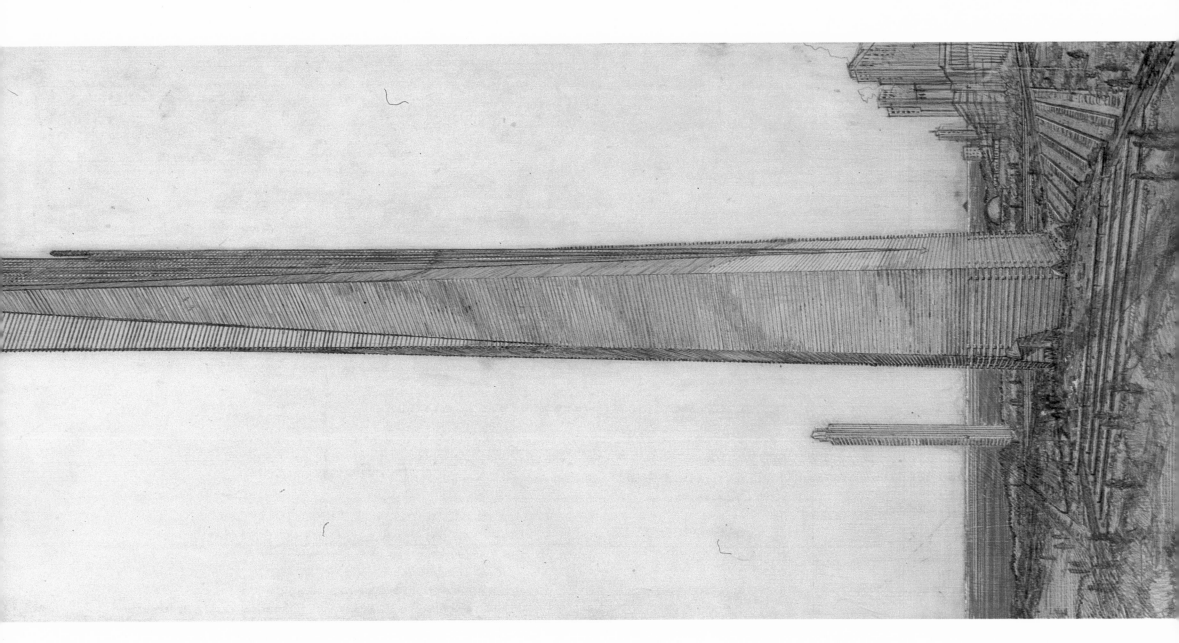

64a

THE MILE HIGH, ILLINOIS, 1956

When Frank Lloyd Wright made his sketches for the Century of Progress (plate 19) to include a fair in a pavilion, another on pontoons, and the third within a skyscraper, he suggested a skyscraper one mile high consisting of 528 stories.

The building was to be primarily a tall structure in line with the principles he had developed so far regarding tall buildings: concrete slab floors cantilevered from a central core that contains stairs, elevators, and utilities; and glass walls protected by metal screens.

On August 10, 1956, he went into the large drafting room at Hillside, near Taliesin in Wisconsin, and made a sketch elevation and a small plan for what he called the Mile High (plate 64a). The elevation shows a rapier-like building, growing more slender as it rises, with a plan based on the form of a tripod. To the left of the sketch he put in an elevation of the Empire State Building of New York, along with the Eiffel Tower in Paris. To the far right he sketched in the Great Pyramid of Cheops at Gizeh, in Egypt. Along the sides of the drawing he printed some basic specifications as follows: "First 20 floors, 18' high, others, 10'. Total rentable area = 6,000,000 square feet; deduct 2,000,000 sq. ft. for high rooms, studios, court rooms, audience halls, etc. Probable cost $60,000,000. Net 4,000,000 sq. ft. @ $10 per sq. ft.; occupancy @ 100 sq. ft. per person = 45,000 persons; transient occupancy in audience halls, etc = 67,000 (approx); total about 100,000 people. Parking 15,000 cars; 100 helicopters. FLLW."

Mr. Wright's son-in-law, William Wesley Peters, who was trained as an engineer and who worked for many years on some of the larger projects such as Fallingwater, the Johnson buildings, and the Guggenheim Museum, suggested to Mr. Wright that he make use of the same structural combination in this new design for the Mile High that he had in the Twin Cantilevered Bridges for Pittsburgh a decade before (plates 44a, 44b). He was referring to Mr. Wright's combined use of the cantilevered floor slab and the steel-in-tension suspension cable at the slab's edge for further stabilization. In this manner, the great weight and bulk necessary to carry and support the structure could be lessened. Mr. Wright immediately adopted the idea, realizing that the more lightweight he could make the building, the safer the building would be. He planned to use plastics rather than glass along with lightweight metals.

During the latter part of August, 1956, word got out that Frank Lloyd Wright had just designed a mile-high skyscraper. The architectural magazines and major newspapers telephoned, each desiring to scoop the project.

Mr. Wright decided to hold off and release the designs to members of the press and to the architectural journals simultaneously. Meanwhile, the perspective was finished, and four elevations and a vertical section as well. On the final section presentation drawing he put down the following:

Memorial To:
Louis H. Sullivan, son of Chicago
First made the tall building tall
Elisha Otis
Inventor of the upended street
John Roebling
First steel-in-tension on the grand scale: The Brooklyn Bridge
Lidgerwood, naval architect
First ocean liner keel. Makes it what it is today.
Coinget and Monier of France
Reinforced concrete. The body of our modern world.
Salutations:
Eduardo Torroja, engineer, Spain
Professors Beggs - Cross, science of continuity
Professor Pier Luigi Nervi, engineer, Italy
Dr. J. J. Polivka, engineer, University of California
Maillart, engineer, Switzerland

Mayor Richard Daley of Chicago designated September 17, 1956, as Frank Lloyd Wright Day. On the morning of that day, the drawings for the Mile High were to be shown in the ballroom of the Hotel Sherman. In preparation for the exhibition, Mr. Wright made a selection of buildings, both built and in the project stage, that would illustrate just what the seeds of this new idea were, where they began, and how they were employed in architecture and engineering.

The entire ballroom was to be used to house the exhibition, which made possible an extensive selection of Mr. Wright's other work. The earliest work shown was a large photomural of the windmill tower, Romeo and Juliet, which he had built for his aunts' Hillside Home School in 1896, his first engineering-architecture, as he called it. Other works included the Imperial Hotel in Tokyo, the various skyscraper designs he had created beginning with the Luxfer Prism Office building in 1895; the Press Building in San Francisco, 1912; the National Life Insurance Company (plate 12); St. Mark's Tower, 1929; followed in 1940 by the grouped towers of the same design, Crystal Heights (plates 24a, 24b); the Rogers Lacy Hotel (plates 36a–36c); the Johnson Research Tower, 1944; and the recently completed Price Tower in Oklahoma.

We, his apprentices, also prepared many other projects and completed buildings for exhibit. But when we drew out a set of working drawings to take down to Chicago, Mr. Wright shook his head and said, "No, boys, no working drawings. How we do it, how we put it together is one cat we are not going to let out of the bag." Taliesin apprentices John Rattenbury, John

64b

Amarantides, and I went down to Chicago and spent several days organizing the exhibit. We could not get into the ballroom until the midnight before the exhibition was to open, so we mounted the show in the hotel warehouse next door. Finally, following a grand wedding reception, at the stroke of twelve we started to move in while waiters and busboys removed debris from the preceding event.

At three o'clock in the morning, the new drawing for the Mile High was driven down by other apprentices. It had been made on a large roll of canvas, twenty-six feet high, on three black and white photomurals made from the eight-foot-tall original drawing. We had stretched out the canvas across saw-horses in the Hillside drafting room, and Mr. Wright began the rendering of the perspective. On the sun side of the building, Mr. Wright had made the lines in bronze and gold inks; on the shade side in silver and blue inks. At the Hotel Sherman we unrolled the drawing and stretched it on a frame that we had made and set it up reaching from table-height almost to the ceiling of the ballroom.

By eight in the morning Mr. Wright arrived, the exhibition was in place, and he was ready for the press. Entering the room from the opposite end, the first sight one beheld was this great twenty-six-foot tall drawing at the far end, rising up along the wall. The blue of the sky was, coincidentally, a perfect match to the blue of the interior of the ballroom, and the effect was one of looking out a great picture window onto Chicago's Lake Front with the Mile High rising magnificently in place, standing as though it had been there for eternity.

But why build an office building one mile high? By means of such a building, with its potential occupancy of 100,000 people, the building could stand in the center of a green park, no longer surrounded by clusters of skyscrapers making a cavern of gloom and darkness below. "No one can afford to build it now," Mr. Wright said, "but in the future no one can afford *not* to build it. This is the future of the tall building in the American City. Level Manhattan to one large green, like Central Park, and erect a few of these well spaced apart and you have the congregation desired by city work and city life, but surrounded with trees, fields, parks and streams."

Later, in a talk he gave to the Taliesin Fellowship on December 30, 1956, just a few weeks after the initial unveiling of the Mile High, he further explained:

> The Mile High would absorb, justify and legitimize the gregarious instinct of humanity. And the necessity for getting together would mop up what now remains of urbanism and leave us free to do Broadacre City. The [modern] city in itself now is incongruous, unclassified, an absurdity throughout. We've had it long ago, but passed it without knowing it, and it is in the way of culture. If America is ever going to have a culture of her own, she's got to dispose of these things she calls her cities now. Cities are only justified at ports or at great concentrations of natural materials. But where human life is concerned there is serious indictment, and a serious impediment. The Mile High is a necessary step in the direction of Broadacre City.

With Mile Highs in place of ordinary skyscrapers, the city dweller would be out on the landscape close to the ground. This setting of humanity near to and in harmony with nature is an important key to understanding what Frank Lloyd Wright designed in the realm of architecture. Out of that association of man with his natural environment, Mr. Wright believed, came a fuller, better-developed human being.

The Mile High aimed at that achievement—to free humans from the dense, high-rise slums of the overcrowded, deadly, polluted city. It aimed to provide them with the necessary space for coming together and for commerce and civic activities, but also to let them live a more beautiful life at the same time. If there exists a message to be gleaned from the Mile High other than its remarkable technological achievements, it is surely that.

The design was more than just the sketching out of a vague dream. Details were carefully considered, from the foundation taproot that plunges into bedrock like the handle of a sword, to the rising structure with its component parts. Translucent and transparent exterior wall surfaces are set well back beneath overhanging visors. This provides the same respect for sun protection that Frank Lloyd Wright honored in all his tall buildings. The elevators are vertical trains five cars tall, run on ratchets like a cog railway, and atomic powered. The elevator towers rise up and out through the surface of the building, since the building itself grows smaller toward the top in a continuous slope. Five levels of covered parking terraces flank the base of the building; the top level is a heliport (plate 64b).

The design expresses height, slender and graceful, crystalline by day, glowing by night. It is modern, technologically feasible, a natural product of the twentieth century. Most important, it is poetic and beautiful, intended to be inspiring and comforting to the human life within and around it.

MUNICIPAL GALLERY, BARNSDALL PARK
LOS ANGELES, CALIFORNIA, 1957

"Sixty Years of Living Architecture" was the title that Frank Lloyd Wright gave to his large architectural exhibition that was assembled in 1950. From 1951 to 1954, it toured Europe, Central America, and the United States. Arthur C. Kaufmann of Gimbels in Philadelphia sponsored the show; in fact, the exhibition was initially his idea. After the show had its premiere in Kaufmann's department store in Philadelphia, it had its European premiere in the Palazzo Strozzi in Florence in May 1951. In 1953, the exhibition was set up on Fifth Avenue in New York, on the site of the Guggenheim Museum, housed in a special pavilion that Mr. Wright designed for the occasion.

In 1954, the exhibition was sent to California for display at the Hollyhock House, by then the property of the Department of Cultural Affairs of the city

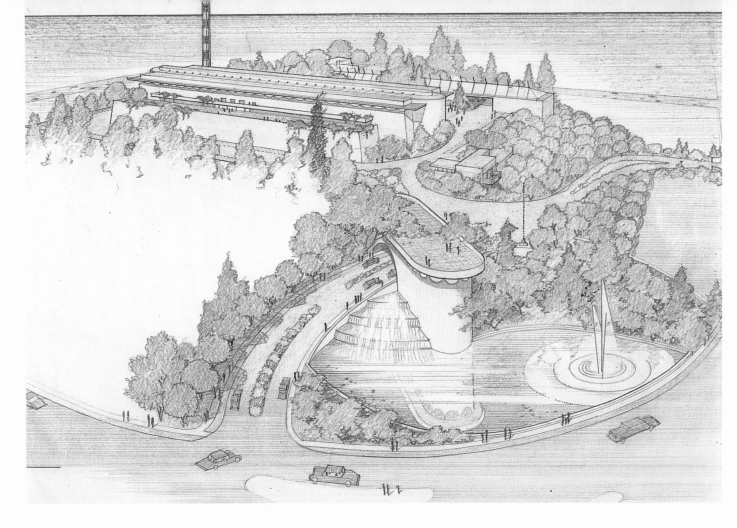

of Los Angeles. Hollyhock House was the residence that Frank Lloyd Wright had designed and built for Aline Barnsdall. It was located on Olive Hill, a grove of olive trees on a hilltop surrounded by a park.

Stretching out from Hollyhock House was a long wing used by Miss Barnsdall as kennels. The pavilion that Mr. Wright designed for the exhibition made use of those kennels. However, it extended them beyond and above by means of the same type of glass and transite panels that Mr. Wright had employed for the pavilion on the Guggenheim site in Manhattan.

Hollyhock House was used for official and cultural receptions by the city. Its art director, Kenneth Ross, who implemented the installation of the exhibition, wanted to have a large permanent art museum on this site for Los Angeles. He approached Mr. Wright with this idea. The plan of the museum as conceived by Mr. Wright (plate 65) utilizes Hollyhock House as its main entrance. It thus directs the public through the house, into the enclosed patio gardens, and then into the entrance of the new museum. The museum building itself is stepped down the hillslope and also provides for several levels of underground parking. The long building, terminated with half circles at either end, has several levels for large galleries, two-story exhibitions, and smaller, more intimate minor galleries.

Entering from the Hollyhock House garden, the public comes directly upon a mezzanine level looking down into the main gallery. The half circles at the ends of the building accommodate sculpture. Ramps proceed along the curved wall from level to level for comfortable access, and allow ample mobility for the handicapped or the infirm. In the top right of the aerial view can be seen the pavilion roof that was built in 1954. The entry drive sweeps up and through an administration wing, which is covered by a large roof terrace. The rectangular building that can be seen between this administration wing and the end of the gallery is Residence A, dating to 1920, part of the original commission for Aline Barnsdall.

The commission for the Barnsdall Municipal Gallery came directly from Ross. He saw clearly the need for a large, city-managed gallery. And since the centrally located Barnsdall Olive Hill property was already owned by the city, it would be most logical to erect a gallery on that site. A group of civic-minded art patrons agreed with him and raised funds out of their own pockets to pay Mr. Wright's fee for the preliminary drawings. However, when they went before the city itself with plans to raise money for the actual building, it soon became obvious that the cost of so large a building would be prohibitive. The project was canceled.

ARTHUR MILLER HOUSE, ROXBURY, CONNECTICUT, 1957

During the final planning stages of the Guggenheim Museum, Frank Lloyd Wright found himself spending so much of his time in New York that the constant renting of rooms at his favorite hotel, the Plaza, became a burdensome expense. Moreover, he needed a New York office, given the amount of time he was spending there. Since he loved the Plaza, he decided to rent a studio-apartment on the second floor. The suite had once been owned by Diamond Jim Brady and Bet-a-Million Gates. When Mr. Wright remodeled it he remarked, "We'll make the apartment Diamond Jim Brady Modern." What he made of that suite was indeed an elegant application of the Mauve Decade, done in rich velvets, black lacquer furniture that we made ourselves at Taliesin, peach-colored wool carpets, walls papered in rice paper panels with speckles of gold leaf, and large circular mirrors with plum-colored wood trim to match the plum-colored velvet draperies.

The Plaza apartment became office and home for Mr. and Mrs. Wright from 1954 to 1959, and they spent a great deal of time there each year. One afternoon, Mrs. Wright went across the street to the Paris Theatre to see a movie. Upon returning, she exclaimed about the actress she had seen for the first time. "You will love her, Frank, she is so talented, vivacious, natural. They cast her in a very sexy role because she is stunning, but the thing you will like best about her is that she is so very natural!" Her name was Marilyn Monroe and the film was *Gentlemen Prefer Blondes*.

In 1957, Mr. Wright received a phone call from the actress, who was at that time married to Arthur Miller, the well-known playwright. She wanted a Frank Lloyd Wright house to be built on a piece of property near Roxbury, Connecticut. An appointment was made, and she came over to the Plaza from her apartment in New York. William Wesley Peters, Mr. Wright's son-

66b

in-law, was in the apartment when the doorbell rang. He opened the door and was astonished to find Marilyn Monroe standing alone at the door asking to see Mr. Wright. Mr. Wright appeared at the door, invited Miss Monroe in, and immediately spirited her into the living room of the suite.

The house that they discussed and that Mr. Wright designed for her was based on the project he had earlier designed for Robert Windfohr in 1949 (plate 52). The property in Roxbury had a slight slope going down to a running brook, and Mr. Wright made that slope a feature of the swimming pool (plate 66b). Naturally, the large, circular living room (plate 66a) provides for a cinema with a projection booth at one end of the area and a film vault. Opposite, in the living room, is provision for a drop-down screen. On the second floor is a large costume vault for Miss Monroe's wardrobe, and provisions are made for a spacious nursery and children's bedrooms. Since Miss

Monroe was anxious to have children of her own, the nursery is an important feature of the upper level plan.

Before work could be started on the house, Marilyn Monroe's life had become increasingly difficult. She separated from Arthur Miller, and the studio complained of her erratic behavior during filming. Her dream to build a Frank Lloyd Wright home for herself and for the children she longed to have was reluctantly abandoned. Her tragic suicide, some years later, grieved all of those who had met her and grown fond of her the several times she visited the Plaza.

It was rare for Frank Lloyd Wright to make a design without first having a direct commission. The challenge that each new work placed before him as a result of definite conditions and limitations—site, needs of the client, and budget—all taken together created the grist for the mill out of which his design flowed naturally. He told us repeatedly that the older he grew the easier the design process became for him. "It is simply a matter of shaking the design out of my sleeve," he said.

A few times in his life he made designs without the prompting of a client asking for something specific. The three schemes he made for the Chicago World's Fair in 1931 (plate 19) were prompted by his desire to create a fair that would survive the actual event and become a permanent architectural contribution. His designs for the Skyscraper Regulation (plates 15a, 15b) were spurred by his recognition of America's urban life, its problems that were becoming intensified daily, and the desire to find a solution that would permit city dwellers to live in finer circumstances. That was also the reason for the design of the Mile High (plates 64a, 64b) which he once called The Illinois since he had a definite site in mind on Chicago's Lake Front area.

Broadacre City, his enormous visionary design or rather group of designs, came about during a lull in his architectural work in 1934. The Depression was on in full force and there were few architectural commissions coming into his office. With a newly founded architectural school in his home and studio at Taliesin, the idea of creating a suburban city came to him as a project to which he and his student apprentices could devote full time, including the making of a large model and several smaller models of particular structures.

In 1957, Arizona planned to add on to its existing state capitol in downtown Phoenix. The proposed design was commonplace. The result would make traffic congestion and parking even more intolerable. At this point, Lloyd Clark, a newspaper reporter with the Phoenix Gazette, telephoned for an appointment with Mr. Wright.

When he was shown into Mr. Wright's canvas-topped office at Taliesin West, some fifteen miles northeast of the city of Phoenix, Mr. Wright greeted him with, "So this is Lloyd Clark." "Yes," replied Clark, "and spelled with 2 L's, just like yours."

They began discussing the newly proposed skyscraper design for the state capitol downtown. "In all of my efforts I have never done anything for the

people whose community I have enjoyed for 25 years," Mr. Wright said. "But I don't run around after work. I'm not a hawker. If I were, the job would have me rather than me having the job."

Reaching for a pencil and a tablet he continued talking to Mr. Clark as he simultaneously made sketches, free-hand, on the paper in front of him. "It would be a great spreading shelter that might resemble a dome—not the conventional dome—serving to shade the building. There would be a broad expanse with gardens and fountains. A capitol in the sun country should not resemble anything in New York City." Meanwhile, a sketch elevation and plan had materialized on the paper, and Mr. Wright handed it to Clark and said, "Why not publish it?" Mr. Clark asked if there were a site in mind and was told, "Nearby Papago Park; it is a beautiful configuration of sculptured hills close enough to Phoenix to be a part of Phoenix, yet open and spacious. It would make an excellent backdrop to the building."

Clark then suggested that rather than publishing anything at present, Mr. Wright make a more formalized drawing and have a presentation either at Papago Park itself or perhaps in a meeting room at the Westward Ho Hotel downtown with the press present. Mr. Wright chose the hotel, and a few weeks later the drawings for the building, which he called Oasis, were on display with Mr. Wright present to explain them. He further named the project Pro Bono Publico, for the public good, and dedicated the design to the citizens of Arizona. He told them:

These preliminary drawings [plates 67a, 67b] indicate a high, wide, sheltering, crenolated, copper-plated, concrete, self-supporting, canopy of modern open construction like a great tree filtering sunlight over subordinate copper roofs over beautiful buildings, gardens, pools, and fountains: beautiful vistas standing together beneath this sheltering canopy. These buildings are there all in harmonious relation to the great hexagonal domed shelter and are so related to each other. Native onyx columns, native stone, native copper—all Arizona materials are employed and well exploited in the great modern ferro-concrete system of construction here used and that is now constituting the twentieth-century body of our world. Created like a true oasis in the desert, here it is sheltered by naturally air-conditioned spaciousness for legislative functions—no vertical jam, no time lost, but all on one level. Direct service, private or public, all free at all times to all points. A new freedom, this, standing in modern terms for Arizona now as the Alhambra once stood for Spain long before our continent was discovered. To build an already dated urban monstrosity to present Arizona to posterity seems to me a crime punishable by you, yourselves! Hoping to save the state—I love the state—from

the egregious error proposed by authority and to rouse you to action, I have put on paper these definite outlines of an edifice more suitable to the character and beauty of the State of Arizona and its unique landscape.

Of course, the plan was rejected as "too ornate" and "too revolutionary, too expensive"—all reasons dredged up by the timid to justify their rejection of any good idea. Years later, Secretary of Interior Stewart Udall was once asked, "Why is it that Arizona, the most beautiful State in the Union, has the ugliest state capitol?" "Because," he replied, "we missed the boat and muffed the ball when we rejected the Oasis project designed by Frank Lloyd Wright."

BAGHDAD CULTURAL CENTER, BAGHDAD, IRAQ, 1957

The designs made for a cultural center for the city of Baghdad in Iraq came naturally to Frank Lloyd Wright out of two sources of inspiration. One was the result of his living in the American Southwest desert for more than twenty-five winters of his life, a climate and ambiance similar to Iraq. The other grew out of his own lifelong love and admiration for the world of Islam, including its characteristic architecture and decorative style. He was initially commissioned to design an opera house for the city of Baghdad, following an invitation from the Cultural Commission of the government of Iraq to fly over and see first-hand the city and the program required. In May 1957, he left Arizona and headed for the Middle East.

As the airplane was coming down for a landing near Baghdad, Mr. Wright saw out the window a long, slender island in the Tigris River. Once through customs he asked who owned that island. It was the property of the royal household, he was told, whereupon he asked to be taken to the king, a man in his early twenties. As he was being introduced to the king, the royal aide announced, "Mr. Wright, His Majesty, the King of Iraq." "And here," Mr. Wright said as he bowed, "is His Majesty, the American Citizen."

He then went on to speak of his commission for the design of the Opera House and how he had noticed a particular island in the Tigris River while flying over the city. When he explained that the island would be a more fitting site for the Opera House than any crowded downtown area, the king leaned over, touched Mr. Wright on the wrist and said, "The island, Mr. Wright, is yours!"

For that island, several cultural buildings besides the Opera House were planned (plate 68a). Included was a civic auditorium, accompanied by a planetarium below and surrounded by a vast series of ramps for easy access and for sheltered parking. Extending down the length of the narrow island would be a museum for the gigantic sculpture of the Middle East—the lions and the man-headed, animal-bodied statues of the Assyrians. Another art museum was planned for the paintings and sculpture of contemporary artists. A grand bazaar was planned with shops and kiosks in the manner of the great open air markets throughout the Moslem world. The terminal of the island was to contain a large sculptural monument to Haroud al-Raschid, legendary caliph of Baghdad, who designed the first city in the form of circles and who in 798 A.D. exchanged ambassadors with the Western world at Aix-la-Chapelle through his friendship with and admiration for Charlemagne.

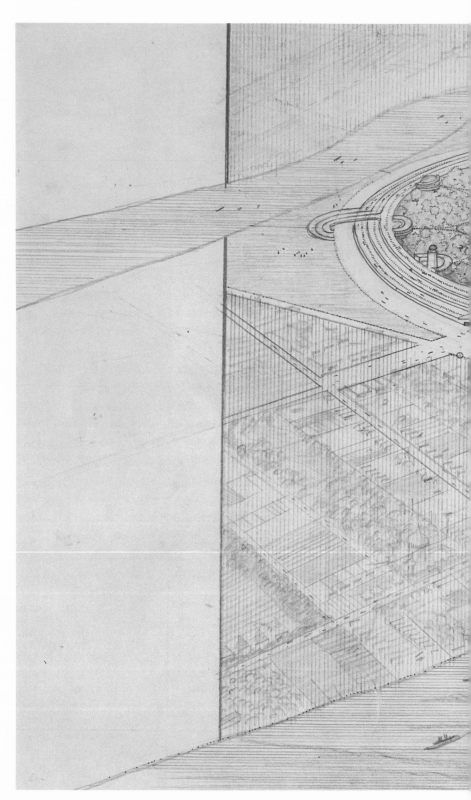

68a

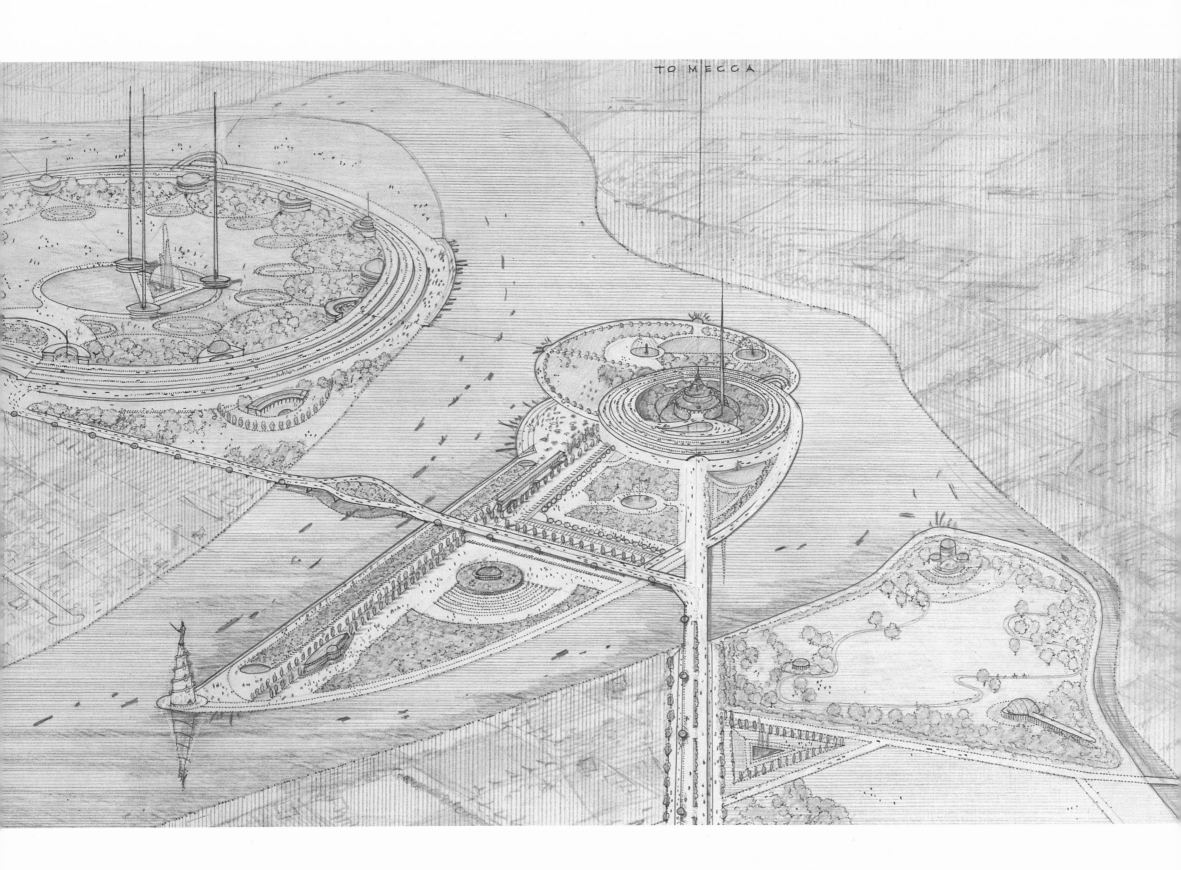

TO MECCA

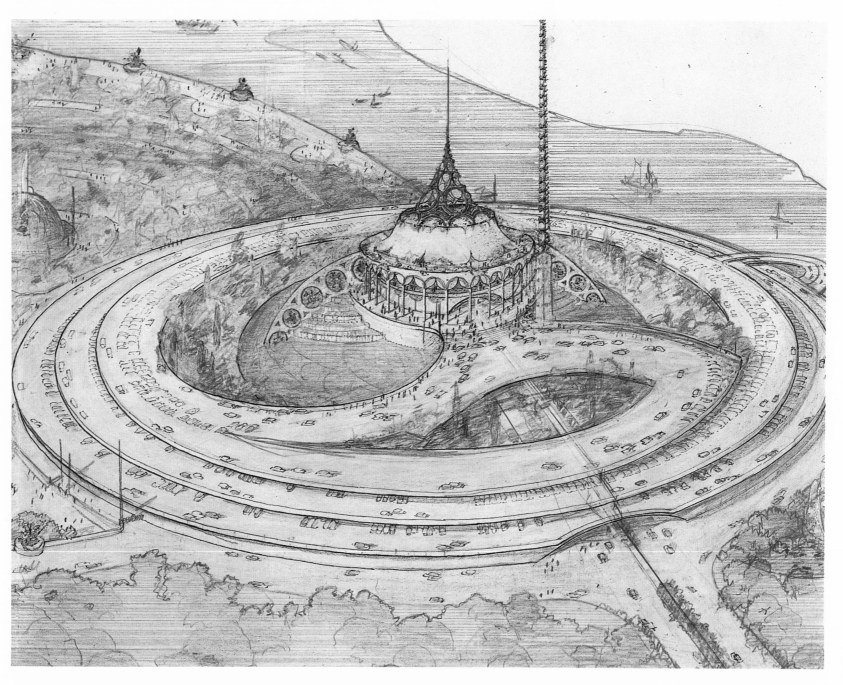

68b

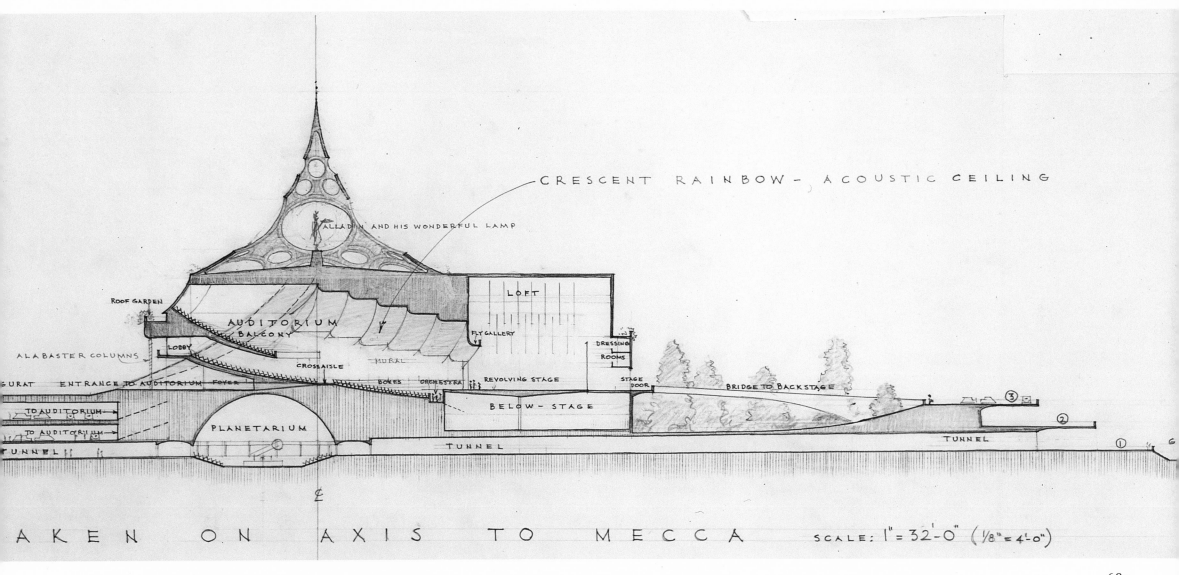

CRESCENT RAINBOW — ACOUSTIC CEILING

ALLADIN AND HIS WONDERFUL LAMP

ROOF GARDEN

LOFT

AUDITORIUM BALCONY

FLY GALLERY

ALABASTER COLUMNS

LOBBY

DRESSING ROOMS

MURAL

CROSSAISLE

GURAT

ENTRANCE TO AUDITORIUM FOYER

BOXES

ORCHESTRA

REVOLVING STAGE

STAGE DOOR

BRIDGE TO BACKSTAGE

TO AUDITORIUM

PLANETARIUM

BELOW-STAGE

TO AUDITORIUM

TUNNEL

TUNNEL

TUNNEL

AKEN ON AXIS TO MECCA   SCALE: 1" = 32'-0" (1/8" = 4'-0")

Across the river on the other bank was planned a large university complex based on the spiral ramp that predominates the design for the Opera House, but much larger in scale. A series of three-tiered highways are likewise stacked to provide shaded parking. All the various buildings of the campus abut the roadway, the central core set as a great park.

For this desert climate, the window areas in all the buildings were kept to a minimum as a protection against the sun. The entire Opera House area (plate 68b) is surrounded by what is labeled on the plan as "Ziggurat," which forms both a driving and a parking area. It is tiered in such a way that the levels produce shade for the parked cars. Separating this great tiered ramp is

a garden with waterfalls and a bufferzone of trees and shrubs between the Opera and the Ziggurat. The Opera House itself is designed to seat three thousand persons. The proscenium continues from within the hall to the outside and contains bronze, sculptured medallions depicting scenes from the famous Thousand and One Nights of Scheherazade. This great arch of medallions borders a series of cascading waterfalls. Beneath the main hall of the Opera House is another large civic building, a planetarium (plate 68c).

Along the great mall that extends from the Opera House at one end of the island to the monument of the caliph at the other, were planned two museums, one a gallery for Mesopotamian sculpture such as the great Assyrian winged bulls, the other (plate 68d) a museum for paintings and sculpture of the more recent eras. This art museum is a long eliptical shape with a circle protruding from the center on one edge to contain the entrance foyer, roofed with a lattice-like pattern of concrete beams and glass. The major gallery within is lit by means of the circular clerestory windows visible on the rendering. Following the periphery of this large gallery is a series of minor galleries.

The ceiling is dome shaped, and rides directly above the ring of clerestory windows. Light is therefore reflected by the ceiling and cast onto the art objects below. In Iraq where the sun is so intense, strong direct lighting is definitely much less desirable than reflected light. In the foyer and throughout the major gallery are recessed pools for sculpture. On the drawing of a cross section, beneath a sunken sculpture pool Mr. Wright wrote the note: "Fountains over sculpture."

The shopping kiosks, in keeping with Moslem tradition for the showing and sales of wares, were ingenious combinations of globelike upper areas set upon cubelike lower areas, the ground level for selling, the spheres above open for the display of merchandise.

The Monument to Haroud al-Raschid is designed to represent a caravan of camels and drivers, proceeding in a continuous spiral until it reaches the top and the gilt statue of the caliph himself.

A year following the presentation of these projects, the government of Iraq was overthrown and the king was brutally murdered. Gone forever was any hope of realizing the Frank Lloyd Wright buildings for the Moslem nation of Iraq.

68d

TRINITY CHAPEL, NORMAN, OKLAHOMA, 1958

Trinity Chapel, as it was to be called at the University of Oklahoma in Norman, was originally commissioned by Mr. and Mrs. Fred Jones. Fred Jones was a car dealer in Oklahoma City who offered to donate a chapel to the university. At one point it was to be called the Jones Chapel. Mr. Wright's original concept design was made on the back of an envelope while he was flying from New York to Phoenix. The remarkable nature of his first sketches is revealed in this particular case (plate 69). Done in blue-colored pencil, it is hardly more than a thumbnail sketch, yet both plan and minuscule view are so precisely drawn that the final presentation drawings seem to be only a blow-up of what was first put down on paper.

The proposed design is a small chapel raised off the ground to provide parking below, the sanctuary approached by outspread ramps for easy access. The walls of the triangular structure rise in masses of poured concrete, perforated for stained glass windows on the three sides. These walls with their panels of stained glass continue to rise to become tower and steeple in one uninterrupted, continuous line. On the bottom of the presentation perspective Frank Lloyd Wright wrote: "To Nature—the Sectless Chapel."

There seemed to be, however, no little misunderstanding about the project. When the drawings were shown to the clients at Taliesin they were somewhat baffled by what Mr. Wright had created. Upon their return to Norman, they expressed their displeasure with the project and Mr. Wright wrote to them:

My dear Mr. and Mrs. Jones! I have completely misunderstood the nature of the commission from you I was happy to receive. I did not know the chapel was an adjunct of the University because you did not tell me so. Your objections are of course in that case understandable.

A chapel without fundamental parking, which is the basis of the design you saw at Taliesin, is entirely something else, and the icing of the ramps is more easily handled than the icing of steps. So I take it what I have done does not please you. Since I have no interest in a conventional chapel you may consider yourselves entirely free to consider the episode closed. I will take my labor for my pains and hope to build the "non-sectarian" elsewhere. Sometime. Sincerely yours—and sorry, Frank Lloyd Wright June 9, 1958

The dedication of this chapel to Nature toward the end of his life is of considerable significance. So many of his later talks to us at Taliesin centered on this continuing theme of the study of Nature, of looking as deeply into Nature as possible. He called the person who pursued this type of study the seer, the philosopher, the poet, the one who seeks the innate character within. This quest grew in importance for Mr. Wright the longer he lived, and as he grew in stature so also he grew in this sense of natural perception. With a profound and all-consuming passion he spoke of the marvelous lessons and principles that Nature showed him and how he perceived they could apply to architecture, not as a copying or imitation of forms but as an application of principles that are universal.

69

TODD A-O THEATERS, 1958

Mike Todd was an impresario who developed and produced a type of cinema projection that made use of a very large screen filled with an equally large, and therefore dramatic, image. He called this form of projection Todd A-O. Cinerama with its broad screen was popular at the same time, but cinerama required three cameras carefully synchronized to project three parts of a single image on one large screen. The weak point in this system was the seam line where the three parts met. Todd A-O did away with that by means of a special lens. It required, however, new projection equipment and new size screens.

Together with Pat Weaver, a former NBC president, and the industrialist Henry J. Kaiser, Todd formed a corporation that intended to build, throughout the country, theaters not only for Todd A-O productions but also for concerts and live theatrical productions.

In December 1957, Mike Todd and his wife, Elizabeth Taylor, came to Taliesin West to commission Frank Lloyd Wright to make the designs for those theaters. Kaiser was then producing the aluminum geodesic domes designed by Buckminster Fuller, and it was the intention of Todd, Weaver, and Kaiser to use these domes as a basic roof for the new theater. Mr. Wright agreed to the idea and kept the design of the Fuller dome but modified its size and the scope of its overhead curve. Rather than start from the ground and form a complete hemisphere, he designed precast concrete shells to serve as walls from which only the upper two-thirds of a dome would rise. This made for a gentler line of curvature (plate 70).

Like most impresarios, Mike Todd lived a whirlwind life. During the four months that negotiations were underway with Mr. Wright, telegrams and quick, darting visits abounded. Speed seemed the essential characteristic of Todd's life. Mr. Wright tried to get him to settle down long enough to look at the designs he had prepared for him. He telegraphed in March: "Dear Mike Todd: You are missing the Michael Todd Universal Theatre. Minneapolis wants one, and South Bend, Indiana another. You shouldn't take what others tell you but see for youself. Love to Elizabeth, but the new Michael Todd is almost as beautiful and will last longer. Frank." There were more delays in forming a meeting, and finally Mr. Wright wired:"Dear Mike: What about the theatre project? Is it dead or are we just not so smart as we thought you were. Frank Lloyd Wright." Todd immediately replied: "Leaving now for San Francisco and New York. Will stop in Phoenix on Friday for conference. Wire New York office if this is agreeable."

He was never to meet with Mr. Wright nor see the drawings that were awaiting him at Taliesin. On his way west, he took a private plane for a personal detour. The plane crashed and Todd was killed.

Weaver telegraphed Mr. Wright soon after, saying that they were still trying to recover from the tragedy. "However, Mike Todd, Jr., Mr. Kaiser and I would like to see the dome plans, if you would send them air mail special delivery to 430 Park Avenue."

Mr. Wright wired back: "Will bring drawings with me to NY. Please call me at the Plaza on Tuesday, April 29th. Affectionate regards, FLLW." The next morning, however, Mr. Weaver wired a request to send the drawings to Mr. Kaiser in Oakland, California. "I am sure that we would all prefer to go over the plans with you personally but this is just not possible at this time," he went on to state.

Mr. Wright replied: "Have never submitted radical scheme by mail and hesitate to do so now. Why not await the normal opportunity. Consider the affair important. Will be here Sunday, April 27, if you can stop over on way West. Frank Lloyd Wright."

Deliberations went on for some time, but the enthusiasm for the project kindled by Mike Todd, Sr., never really spread to the others. There were arguments over size, details of stage construction, and the use of fly-loft. Interest in the project gradually faded. Finally it was dropped altogether.

Out of the project, however, came two important concepts. One was for a small but expandable theater of six hundred seats which could include an option for a larger hall to house fifteen hundred. It was originally planned for prefabrication and mass production. The second concept called for movie theaters all over the nation to be built adjacent to shopping centers, so that the evening parking space of daytime stores could be used by the community attending the cinema. The concepts to which this project gave birth have become commonplace parts of our present culture.

DONAHOE TRIPTYCH, PARADISE VALLEY, ARIZONA, 1959

The last drawing to bear Frank Lloyd Wright's signature is this home intended for a small mountaintop near Phoenix. Helen Donahoe had called upon Mr. Wright in March 1959 asking if he would come into Paradise Valley, not far from his own Taliesin West, and look at a building site she had acquired. Mr. Wright drove down to meet the client and to see the property first hand. The previous owner had bulldozed the top of the mountain to make a flat level where there had once been a peak, thus destroying the mountaintop itself. Mr. Wright at first assumed that Mrs. Donahoe wanted to build a modest-sized cottage somewhere on the lower slopes of the steep hillside, but she told him instead that she wanted a large house on the top. "Very well," Mr. Wright replied, "then we will have to put the top back on the mountain!" That is exactly what the design accomplished.

Mrs. Donahoe wanted a winter home that would accommodate not only herself but also have provision for two complete additional dwellings. These houses would be for members of her family to live in when they came to visit her. The main house, placed on the flat level top, contains the largest portion of the scheme, but bridges span out in two directions to link the two other smaller residences to the central one (plates 71a, 71b). These other homes could be run as independent

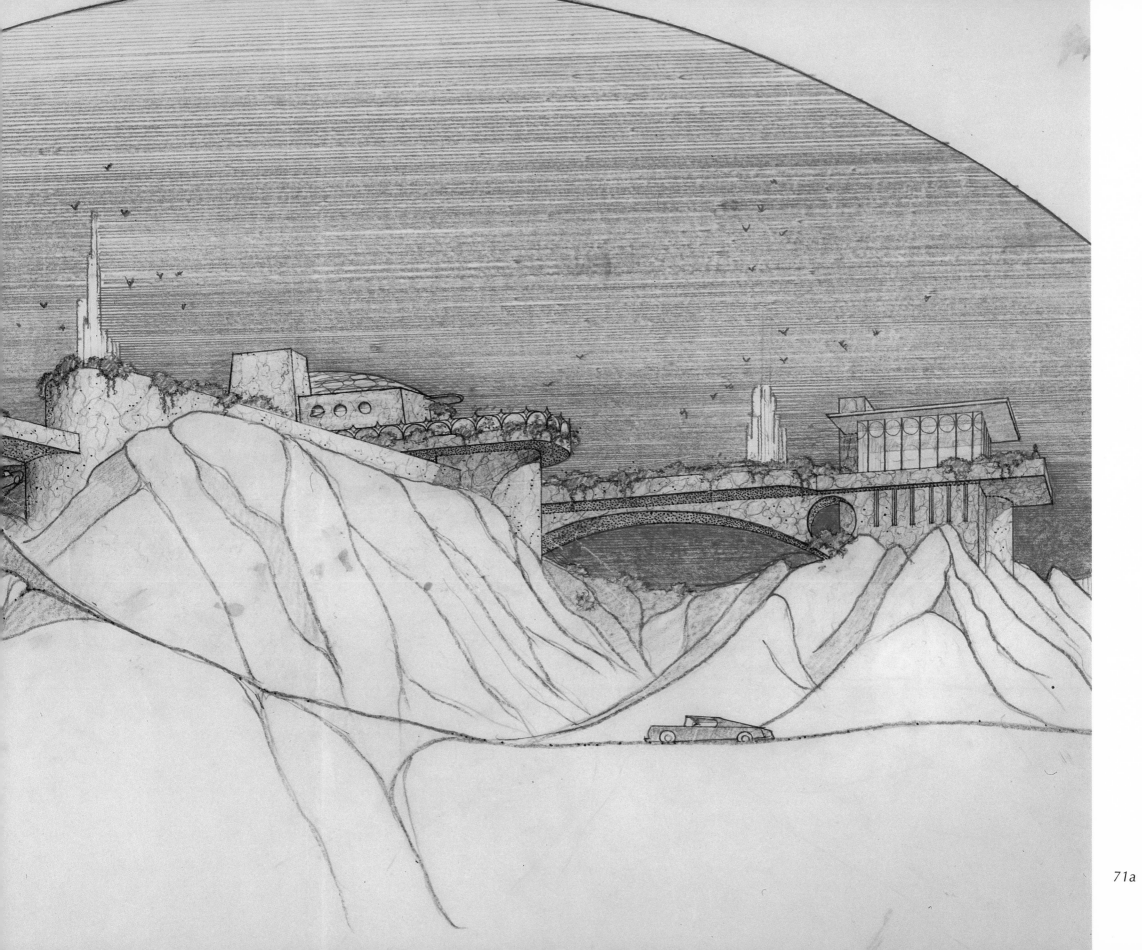

71a

establishments with living-dining spaces, kitchens, bedrooms, and baths. The large, central house has more amenities and provides room for extensive entertaining. The top level contains what is called the Sky Parlor, a domed living room with a view 360 degrees from the mountaintop. An exterior ramp gives access to this living room as well as to interior stairs and an elevator. A large dining room on the level below opens onto a screened terrace with fountains and a swimming pool. A retaining wall in the car court, composed of a desert masonry construction held by concrete, actually wraps up from the hill slope and over to form a roof for the carport. The automobiles are thereby concealed by the curving wall, as though placed under a segment of frozen surf. Mr. Wright poetically named the grouping the Donahoe Triptych.

However, Helen Donahoe was not as anxious to build as she had led her architect to believe. Mr. Wright died on April 9. Mrs. Donahoe waited several months before paying for the preliminary drawings. After much pressure, she paid only a small percentage of what she owed. It is unfortunate that this project remains unbuilt, for these three lovely residences joined together, appearing to be in harmonizing flight off the mountain crest, compose the last design by Frank Lloyd Wright.

LARKIN BUILDING, BUFFALO, NEW YORK, 1906

Early in his career, Frank Lloyd Wright had two clients who became very close personal friends. They helped him in many ways, with personal advice, business counseling, and often financial assistance. They paid for his trip to Florence in 1909, when he went to live in Italy for a year for the preparation of the great monograph of his work published by Ernst Wasmuth in Berlin. Both men were prosperous in business as well as privately wealthy.

One was Francis W. Little, who built a house by Mr. Wright in Peoria in 1900 and then a second home for a summer residence on Lake Minnetonka, near Minneapolis. (The living room of the Minneapolis house has been purchased and reassembled in the American Wing of the New York Metropolitan Museum.)

The other early friend and patron was Darwin D. Martin. Martin became co-owner of the Larkin Company, a mail-order house operating out of Buffalo, New York. He built not only the ill-fated Larkin Building in Buffalo (demolished in 1950 to make room for a parking lot) but also a large home, now part of the State University at Buffalo, and a summer home on Lake Erie—all designed by Mr. Wright. For more than thirty-five years, he kept his faith and support as a constant friend and patron. "Give me an enlightened businessman," Mr. Wright professed, "and I can change the face of the nation." No one better fitted that definition than Darwin D. Martin.

Why, one might ask, include the Larkin building (plate 72) in a book devoted to projects, to buildings that were never built? The Larkin building was, after all, constructed in Buffalo in 1906. It is included here because it is unquestionably the building that has exerted the most influence in the world of modern architecture. It is to twentieth-century architecture what the ambulatory of St. Denis was to Gothic architecture in the year 1147. It is the great form-giver and innovative pioneer from which modern architecture grew. With few exterior windows, the general light source came from an overhead skylight on the sixth floor that poured light down into a central court. All the floors were designed as balconies overlooking the court, each floor level with its own window area but using a minimum amount of exposed glass surfaces. Light was controlled to be pleasant, not glaring. In an industrial area no outside view is of any value; therefore, the building turned into itself just as the Johnson Administration building and the Guggenheim Museum would do. The inner court served as the focal view including its conservatory-garden-restaurant on the top level.

The materials of the building were brick and reinforced concrete, and the building made no attempt at decoration other than what integrally belonged to the structure.

It was designed to be a completely modern twentieth-century office building, one in which the interior environment would be conducive to pleasant working conditions. Air conditioning was here used for the first time. Fresh air from the roof was brought down through sealed shafts to the basement, and there forced through moistened cotton filters to cleanse it. It then passed over clear, clean water and came up into the building for cooling.

All office furniture was made of steel with magnesite panels, the first metal office furniture. Filing cabinets were designed so that documents were held vertically, rather than the customary drawers with flat stacks that had been used up to that time. In water closets the toilets were wall hung, to facilitate cleaning the floors. The doors to the office building were simple sheets of plate glass, held by dowel-like pins at the top and the bottom.

The Larkin company did not separate offices. The general work area was on the ground floor for the main executives, their secretaries, and staff. Balconies contained further office space, with provisions for closed conference rooms as needed. As early as 1906, the company initiated the idea of the morning and afternoon tea and coffee breaks, at which time both employers and employees gathered together at the top-level conservatory-restaurant. There, tea and coffee were served within a gardenlike atmosphere while music was played on a pipe organ in the restaurant.

Unnecessary ornament was stripped away. Materials were used according to their intrinsic nature. All the technology of the twentieth century was put to full advantage to create a monolithic building whose form and shape expressed its interior space. Here was an explicit advocate of the idea of "from within outward." Nothing extraneous was applied, nothing pretentious, no harking back to archaic European styles and fashions.

This building had a vast influence on the new generation of architects in Germany, Holland, and Belgium. "The two things that impressed me most during my visit to America were Wright's Larkin Building at Buffalo and the Niagara Falls," wrote the state architect of Holland, E. P. Berlage, in 1917. The early work of the modern architects in Europe reflected that influence, an influence that eventually was to come back into the United States some thirty years later by way of the German Bauhaus, as the International Style. But with the International Style, the very precepts of organic architecture were lost.

The signs and symbols of the industrial revolution lay all around the Larkin building in glaring ugliness. The building rose out of this vicious environment as though in spite of it. Standing alone, it showed the twentieth century what its great technological benefits, its miracles of modern materials, could produce by way of a building in which indoor working conditions for both labor and management were more comfortable and inspiring than had ever existed before.

This building's demolition continues to be a grievous blow to the world of architecture. Now it remains for another enlightened client to come forward and build it. The Larkin Building's original working drawings still exist. Its concepts and their practical application—like all of the work of Frank Lloyd Wright—have such universal appeal that they are at once appropriate and timeless.

72